Praise for **Day Laughs**
Night Cries: Fifteen

"It has the rhythm of the sea."
-Jane Goltz, Editor

"Peaches D. Ledwidge is a voice of survival... that makes
sense out of some of the starkest and harshest realities,
emotional and otherwise that a child could face."
—Lillian Allen, Juno Award-Winning International Dub
Poet

"This powerful story of a young girl's struggle to survive
and find her place in the world will at first break your
heart, but, by the story's end, will mend it again."
— Linda Jackson, author of *The Lie That Binds*

Day Laughs
Night Cries: Fifteen

Peaches D. Ledwidge

To invite the author for lectures, seminars or workshops, or to obtain written permission to use any part of this book, contact Peaches D. Ledwidge or visit Day Laughs, Night Cries Website at www.daylaughsnightcries.com.

1. Creative nonfiction. 2. Mother-daughter relationships-creative nonfiction. 3. Teenagers-coming of age-creative nonfiction. 4. Love-creative nonfiction. 5. Women and girls creative non-fiction. 6. Cancer – Terminally ill nonfiction. 7. Trial – assault. 8. Trauma 8. Religion. I. Title

National Library and Archives Cataloging in Publication has been applied for.
LCCN2012952853

Cover design by Jeannie Reush
www.willdesignforchocolate.com

Author picture by Jay Martin
www.jaymartinphotography.com

®

Day Laughs, Night Cries and the logo are trademarks.

"...weeping may endure for a night,
but joy comes in the morning."
Psalm 30: 5

*Healing wounds,
one teardrop at a time*

Content

PART THREE: ACROSS THE SEA

Acknowledgements

There's a saying that "it takes a village to raise a child," but I don't know if anyone ever mentioned that it takes more than a village to write one book. The people who helped to make my story into a book come from different parts of the world, different cultures, and racial backgrounds. This book would not have as many flavors and as much depth without your generous contribution.

Thanks to the Ontario Arts Council in Canada for the grants that boosted my drive to complete *Day Laughs, Night Cries: Fifteen.*

Thanks to Professor Guy Allen for encouraging me to develop my writing voice and for helping me to flesh out this story in his writing class even though this story was not my first choice.

Thanks to the former Erindale Writers Group (Guy Allen was one of the founding members) where I developed my writing craft for many years. Special thanks to the following members for substantial edits: Kwai-Yun Li, John Currie, Lynn Tremblay, and Tracey Gonneau. Also, thanks to Karen Graham, Rosa Veltri, Laurie Kallis, Adam Giles, Sapna Jain, Bayan Khatib for feedback. Thanks to the other members, whose names I have not mentioned.

Thanks to Rosena Joseph for listening to me as I edit the many drafts over the years I spent writing.

Thanks to Stephanie Sauve, Paulina Rejniewicz, Huamei Han, and Chantal Onge, my peer editors at OISE (University of Toronto) who provided me with feedback when this book was just an embryo, possibly cells. And, Chantal, you said my short story sounded like a novel and I took your word and wrote this book.

Thanks to Lucie Costin-Hall for encouragement.

Thanks to Jennifer Day for content edits that helped me to reorganize the entire book and thanks to Alan

Rinzler for developmental edits that made the story stronger.

Thanks to Kathy Yearwick, at Wilmington University and Susan Perloff, founder of the Philadelphia Writers Group, for editing some of the earlier chapters.

Thanks to my newly found blogger friends I met through my own blog who have helped me to finish this final draft. Thanks for your encouraging comments. Jane Goltz, thanks for your speedy and exceptional copy editing skills and for making me feel *comfortable*.

Thanks to Sonia Senior-Martin for your edits, for always encouraging me to take this book to another level, and suggesting that I revert to the original version.

Thanks to Marie Ekeye for always helping with last minute edits.

Thanks to my Mother (now deceased), who loved me in the many ways she could.

Thanks to my sisters, Paulette, Michelle, Barbara (Junie), for love and support. Barbara, with your assistance, you've helped me to understand more than I would ever know. Melissa, my niece, you're so young and full of wisdom – thanks for allowing me to "drive you crazy" about this work.

Thanks to Danier who is forever teaching me about the joy and challenges of motherhood.

Thanks to my two stepchildren, Ghia and Geoffrey, for your keenness to see the ending of the book and even trying desperately to shed tears so I could take pictures for the book cover and logo.

Thanks to my amazing husband and partner, Geoffrey, for your continued support, encouragement, and editing tips. Thanks for helping me to make this dream a reality.

Author's Note

Dear Readers,

Unearthing memories is sometimes difficult. It's like digging for gold. Memories are sometimes right at the surface, like gold not deep in the ground, and that's why you dig deeper as you search for more. Some memories come by surprise, when you least expect them. They may come rough and dirty, requiring a lot of work. Other memories come dispersed, fragmented, and we can only connect them by a link, through research, or with the help of others. As if we are archaeologists, we put the pieces together.

Day Laughs, Night Cries: Fifteen is a creative nonfiction work based on my experiences and fragments of my memories as I remember them or as they were told to me. I have taken the liberty of using the stories others told me to recreate the events before my birth and in my (very early) formative years. For privacy, the names of the characters, except the main one, have been changed. Also, for the same reason, the names of some of the places have been changed.

I write in Standard English to tell the story, but in Jamaica, for example, some people do not consistently use Standard English. Therefore, the dialogue used in this book is not always word for word. I do not proclaim to remember all that was said, but I've written dialogue with the best of intentions to reveal the truth.

And, of course, this is not the entire story of my life, but it's part of my story, the pieces I elected to tell.

DEDICATION

I dedicate this book to my family who finds love and joy
despite the disharmony in life.

In deepest memory and forever in my heart:
My mother, Evelyn
Sister, Marcia
Brother, Jeffrey
Nephew, Omar

PART ONE
FIFTEEN

1

The Silence

I didn't plan to hate Mama, but now I hate her. I hate her for caging and protecting me too much, hate her for distrusting me, hate her for taking away the joy that once flowed from that place in her and me where she made both of us laugh. Made me laugh deep in my belly, laugh, until water dripped from my eyes, laugh until I coughed, and laugh until I scrambled for water to drink. Now I hate her.

Mama nags me all the time.

"Don't have a boyfriend," she says, as if there were nothing else in the world to worry about.

I roll my eyes, not letting her see.

"Wait until you get to Canada."

I like to mimic her, of course, only in my mind, because kids here are not supposed to talk back to their parents. They must have respect.

Wait until you get to Canada.

"You're playing with fire."

So bring the water.

"You will get pregnant and your life will mash-up here."

Let me mash-up my own life.

"Robert is good-for-nothing."

I close my eyes to shut out her voice, the echoes in my mind. I want Mama to leave me alone.

It's none of her business what I do with my life. For all I know, there's no guarantee that I'll ever get out of Jamaica, so I don't know if I'll ever see Canada. "A promise is a comfort to a fool." That's what Granny used to say many times before she died, and I believed her.

I roll on my belly. "Ughhh!" I dig my face into my pillow. I pray Mama will disappear.

~~◆~~

I hate some of the women in Hector's River too. They are spies. They offer Mama bad news and gossip. They watch me. They talk about me. They cluster and buzz like bees in a hive. Their gossip spreads through Hector's River like wildfire through a parched forest. Their stories, like snakes' bites, poison our minds and sting like nettle when Mama confronts me with what she has heard.

Nights, in my bed, when I think the most, the spies' voices crowd my mind. Mornings, before I rise, I hear their voices too, sending their venom.

"Your daughter was talking to the boy."

"They were holding hands."

"She's getting out of hand."

"She's not a Christian any more."

"She's going to bring you a baby."

"She's too young to have a boyfriend."

"Punish her."

"Beat her. Beat her real good."

I'm tired of listening to too much about me, tired of denying what people say about me, and I'm tired of trying to make Mama believe I didn't go somewhere with Robert. Mama believes every story the women tell her. Their stories build a wall between Mama and me. We fight. We fight without words. Our silence, so loud I'm sure Mama hears my voice in her head as I hear hers in mine, and our bodies, the way we pass, tell each other we cannot touch. That way I keep her at bay.

That's the killer, the silence, killing her, killing me. It's killed our fond moments. Still, I know without a doubt that deep—deep, deep in her soul—I know she loves me. But I don't care. I don't see the world the way she does. She's old, forty-three. Oh yeah. Old people forget what it's like to be young.

~~◆~~

It's another school day, a cloudless morning before I leave the house and Mama starts another monologue.

"If you don't listen, you will feel," she says, "and when you feel, you will learn. Mark my word." Mama plods from my room.

Mama's threats play and play like damaged vinyl records on a turntable. Oh! I want to turn off Mama's volume. Forever!

I trudge to school, thinking about my life, but my mind is like a crowded marketplace with everything and everyone. Too many thoughts. Thoughts about the spies, Mama, the church, school, and now Robert.

Mama should tell the old, nosy spies to watch their own children.

On my way to school, I cuss one woman that I used to respect. She's now an old spy for Mama. She claims I'm not the girl I used to be. She told Mama that I have a boyfriend. Even if I had a boyfriend, it's none of her business.

I say to the old spy, "Go to hell and stop watching me because I didn't hire you to be my watchdog."

The old spy flies to Mama before I get home. I'm not surprised. Not knowing what to say when I bump into her, the old spy says, "That child of yours has no manners."

"You don't have respect for Aunt Cela?" Mama says.

I don't answer.

"You keep acting like a big woman," Mama says, "and I'll set you straight. You need a good beating."

~~ ♦ ~~

As Mama and her old spies have already put me on trial and passed the verdict that I have a boyfriend, I'm getting used to being a convict. They think that because I talk to Robert, I've selected him as my boyfriend. I don't even like Robert. He's three years older than I am and he's not the type of boy I want to marry because I'm a Christian and he's not. All the Christians in Hector's River say never marry someone who is not a Christian or else they'll pull you to hell with them. I don't want to go to hell.

Robert walks beside me as I walk from church beside my eighteen-year-old sister, Shernette, who is the same age as Robert.

"I'm sorry for you," Shernette says. "Seems like you can't get rid of him."

Just before Shernette and I step into a pool of light under one of the light-posts, walking in this ungodly way, of course, with Robert by my side like my twin, Robert stops me. He grips my wrist to prevent me from walking away. I wriggle my hand to free it from his hold. It hurts, so I relax.

"Let me go, Robert. Jesus is my man."

"Come on, I can be your second man. Shernette, tell your sister I like her. Tell her to talk to me."

"I can't tell her what to do." Shernette says and walks away. "Leave her alone if that's what she wants."

Oh dear, the old spy again. Her eyes, big and bright in this night, rest on me. She passes by.

"Please, let me go, Robert. There are rumors that you're my boyfriend."

"Ignore the old people. If they want to talk, give them more to say."

It's about a month since Robert has been holding my hand and pestering me to be his girlfriend. And I have given him the same answer—that Jesus is my man—but Robert is like a stubborn stain Mama can't wash out of a piece of clothing. He doesn't care what I say, he will not take no for an answer, and he will not go away.

"But I can't have two men, Robert."

"Course you can." Robert tickles my palm with his other hand.

What is this feeling?

I once had a boyfriend. Grant, yes, that was his name. We were eleven and we were sixth-grade classmates. He was supposed to be my future husband, but a bully in the classroom caused me to give up my future husband when she discovered I loved Grant. I stopped talking to Grant and he didn't know why. But he didn't pester me when I ignored him, and he didn't tickle my palm the way Robert does. Maybe it's because we were young. I don't know.

I'm starting to like Robert because he tickles my hand. He's mixed Indian and African and I'm mixed African and maybe Syrian. My oldest sister, Rose, who lives in Canada, said that after the British got rid of slavery, they went to Ireland, Syria, India, China and some other places to find workers. They took people to work on sugar plantations as indentured laborers because the British were not allowed to bring any more Africans from Africa to Jamaica. This is why almost everyone, including Robert, is so mixed up in Jamaica.

"I have to go," I say. "Shernette is probably home now."

"Let me walk with you. It's dark," Robert says.

"People are going to talk."

"Let them talk." Robert ambles with me, arm brushing against arm. I worry that Mama will hear this bad news.

2
The Side Door

At home, on the veranda, I ask Shernette what she thinks about Robert, and she says he's OK, that he seems nice but a little pushy. My other sister, Andrea, who is older than Shernette, doesn't mind Robert. I tell my sisters that I'm starting to like Robert.

"Be careful," they say.

As I walk in the house, Mama says, "Why did you take so long to come home?"

"I was walking slowly."

"You were with that boy. I keep telling you," Mama says, "if you can't hear, you will feel, and when you feel you will learn."

~~ ◆ ~~

Robert and I meet more and more, despite Mama's threats. Shernette likes him a little, Andrea likes him a lot, but Mama hates him totally.

Some nights Mama stays at Mr. Isaac's house. Mr. Isaac is Bridgette's father. Bridgette is my younger sister. Before Mama leaves the house I pretend I'm asleep or that I'm about to sleep. Robert and I wait for Mr. Isaac to take Mama on his bike. When the sound of the bike fades, Robert walks onto the veranda, and I jump out of bed and tell Shernette and Andrea I'll meet Robert outside.

This night is the third time Robert meets me in my yard. We trek to our favorite spot at the back of the house. Robert and I sit on the back steps, near the door. I had never before noticed how beautiful and colorful the stars are and how gracefully they shoot across the sky with their silver trails of silver lights.

We enjoy the night cries from God's creatures and creation: crickets, dogs, cats, and the sea. The cool sea breeze strokes my face. I like my new life more. We talk and talk, and we say goodbye. Before I sleep, I pray and ask God to forgive me for being outside with Robert. But even after praying, the guilt stays with me, and I dream that God has come for his people, and has left me behind.

~~♦~~

The bike engine booms outside the gate. The bikers, Mama and Mr. Isaac, have arrived. They barge into the house. The bikers stop in Shernette's room before entering mine. Chaos begins.

"I can't trust this child any more," Mama says in a loud, displeasing voice.

"Can't trust her," Mr. Isaac says.

Trust issue with Mama confirmed. I can't trust myself, either.

"If you leave this house another night when I'm not here," Mama says and points her finger at me, "you're going to see who is the woman in this house."

I wonder why Mama thinks I want to be the woman of this house.

Mama gives me the evil eye and says, "If I hear about you and that boy again, you'll see."

Mama and her man stomp from the room, and I wonder what they'll do next. With one glance at Shernette's smirking face, I know. Mama's spy list grows, and now my own sister works against me. I can't believe this is happening. The situation as I see and feel it in this house is getting—what's the word?—critical: scary threats, deadly stares, and terrifying dreams. What else?

Shernette had promised to keep my secret about Robert.

"Why did you tell on me?" I turn to Shernette.

"Mama used to beat me when I talked to my boyfriend," she says. "You used to tell on me, too."

"Geez, but you told me it was OK. If you never did, I wouldn't have let him come into the yard."

I didn't tell on Shernette because she had a boyfriend. I told on her because she skipped school to visit her boyfriend who lived in another village, and I thought she needed to stay in school. But I guess it doesn't matter why I did it. I betrayed her. "What goes around comes around." That's what people in this village say.

Still, I hate Shernette for reporting to Mama. I will talk to her only if I have to.

I run to Andrea next door.

"Andrea, I know you didn't do it."

"Do what?"

"Tell on me."

"No. Why?"

"Cause I met Robert when Mama slept at Mr. Isaac's house last night. She said if I leave the house when she's not home again, I'll know who the woman of this house is."

"Be careful," Andrea says.

The door from my room to Andrea's room leads me through Andrea's back door and to Robert. This is the only way I can see Robert at nights again.

"Can I walk through your side door, Andrea?"

"I'll get in trouble if I let you do that."

"They won't know, Andrea."

~~ ◆ ~~

Night. The bike's noise dies in the distance. With a great plan that Mama won't ever suspect and Shernette who will be too sleepy to detect my plot, I can see Robert. I sneak through the side door and out Andrea's back door and meet Robert. The rush to see Robert and the fear that Shernette or Mama could catch us is wonderfully scary. They'll never know. Thanks to them for making me think of creative ways to meet Robert. Even though they'll never know, I must be cautious and spend less time with Robert.

Robert waits for me on the back steps. "Why did you walk this way?" Robert says.

I share the news about Mama knowing about our night meetings.

"Mama says you'll mash-up my life," I say to Robert.

"That's not true. She doesn't want me to talk to you. That's all. Don't listen to her."

"I won't."

I share the new plan about my side door and Andrea's back door.

Our meeting is brief. I gently open Andrea's unbolted back door. I wave to Robert and close the door behind me.

Andrea is asleep.

With my eyes wide open, I watch for walls as I tiptoe through Andrea's room, my hands guiding my way because I do not want to bump into something and awake Shernette. I reach for the side door. I turn the lock and pull open the door and it squeaks, but just a little. I tiptoe into my room. I quietly lie on the bed and pull the cover over me.

The next day, the two old bikers storm into the room again. What now? I think. My heart jumps and beats rapidly as Mama and Mr. Isaac appear as if they are ready for battle.

What's my punishment?

3
Hammers and Nails

Mama and Mr. Isaac pound on Andrea's door. The pounding rattles the bolt and door hinges. Sleepily, Andrea opens the door. She rubs her eyes and brushes her face with her hands. Mama faces Andrea. Mama seems ready for a fight because I've never seen her this angry in a long time.

"What?" Andrea says in a dream-like voice.

"You're a bad influence on your sister. You should know better."

"Yes, you should know better," Mr. Isaac says.

Andrea stares at him and then looks at Mama. "Know what?"

"You're giving your sister to a man. Is that all you can do for her? Do you want her to destroy her life like yours?"

I jump from the bed and cover my ears.

"You're older," Mama says and gawks at Andrea and then at me.

I slowly back out of my room and listen from the kitchen.

"What kind of sister are you? Do you want her to end up like you were at fifteen… with a baby? Is that what you want for her?"

"She does what she wants," Andrea says.

"But you let her walk through your door to see that boy."

"You shouldn't do that," Mr. Isaac says.

I want to tell Mr. Isaac to stay out of the conversation because if he wasn't carrying Mama on the back of his bike to his house, I could not see Robert at nights.

Andrea knows something is about to happen. Her eyes turn sad. She looks at Mama with her eyes saying, "Forgive me."

Mama points at Andrea and, in the calmest voice I've heard lately, says "Find your own place. I don't want you living here any more."

"I didn't do anything," Andrea says, "but it's OK. If you want me to leave, I'll leave. "I'll find my own place." Tears roll down her face.

I squeeze my eyes to shut out the sad look on Andrea's face and the mad look on Mama's face.

"What have I done?" I say in my mind. "I'm sinful. Awful. Bad. What have I done to Andrea?"

Mama marches from Andrea's doorway, slams the side door behind her, and plods toward me.

"We have to nail up the door," Mama says to Mr. Isaac.

"Yes, nail up the door," Mr. Isaac says.

God, I can't stand him. He's like Mama's big shadow and a nagging echo.

"This will stop her from sneaking out of the house in the night," Mama says and gives me the evil eye. "I can't trust you any more."

"Can't trust her," Mr. Isaac says.

Listening to Mama and her shadow-echo is irritating. They must be bluffing. "Nail up the door?"

~~ ◆ ~~

Minding my own business. Sitting at the dining room table close to the side door. Working on my English homework. The late evening brings a strange sight: Mama and Mr. Isaac barge into the house and my room. They have gone insane. They have things in their hands. I glimpse two hammers, nails and some planks. Will they build a cage for me? No. I now remember what they had said, but I thought such ideas only lived in people's thoughts. They could not be real, but they're serious. As much as I can't or don't want to believe what I'm seeing, I cautiously watch and listen, but pretend as though I don't care.

Mama and Mr. Isaac pick up their hammers and nails and planks. They stand at each side of the wooden doorframe leading to Andrea's room. They move in a builder's dance—if there's anything like that—every movement in sync as they place one plank across the doorway and hold their nails in place. They hammer long nails into the planks and the doorframe.

Bang!
Bang!
Bang, bang!
Bang!

Mama and Mr. Isaac hammer and hammer. They hammer hammers against nails. They pound and pound in my ears. They mutter and mutter words that sound like chants.

"Good."

"Good."

"Bad child."

"Bad child."

If I could, I would strangle them.

"We-must-nail-up-the-door. Good." Mr. Isaac chews his words together.

Bang. Bang. Bang, bang.

"She's getting out of hand," Mama huffs.

Bang. Bang. Bang, bang. Bang.

I wish the hammers would fall on their toes or that they would drive the nails into their fingers or pound their fingers with their own hammers. I certainly would not call for a doctor.

Bridgette watches. I don't know what she's thinking, but she opens her mouth and gapes. Shernette stands at the doorway leading to the bathroom. She stares, too. I gawk at her and close my eyes tightly and open them—a deliberate, slow, angry squeeze of my eyelids—a "cut-eye," as Jamaicans say.

"This will stop her from sneaking out in the night," Mr. Isaac says.

"She's getting slack. Too slack."

"Girl child mustn't behave like this." Mr. Isaac hammers a nail into the plank on the other side.

Bam, bam, bam.

"She is a disgrace," Mama mutters.

"This will keep her in. This will keep her in."

I wonder how long Mama and Mr. Isaac think they can keep me behind these wooden bars. I don't care whose idea it is to put boards across the door like there is a big storm coming. All I know at this moment is that I hate Mr. Isaac, like I hate Mama. Mama had said many times that, "The upholder is as

16

bad as the doer." I am sure that Mr. Isaac gave Mama the nails, hammers, and the boards, because I saw them at his house. And I know that Mama doesn't have money to buy them.

I work on my English homework, but my mind works more on the nails, the hammers, and the planks. I tell myself that no nails, no hammers, and no planks can cage me. And because "the damage is already done," as Granny used to say, I have nothing to lose any more. Andrea will be gone. My soul is gone to the devil. I'm a caged bird, and everyone in this house already thinks that I'm bad. Now I'll do whatever I want. Mama and Mr. Isaac plod from the room with their hammers hanging from their hands.

"You go on," Mama says. "I've been telling you, if you don't listen, you will feel, and when you feel, you will learn. You need a good beating."

Andrea says she'll take Owen to live with his dad, Steve, who lives in Trench Town, Kingston, and she asks Mama to give her some time to move. Mama gives her a month, but tension grows high in this house. I don't talk to Andrea when Mama is around. Andrea doesn't talk to Mama, and Mama doesn't talk to Andrea. I don't talk to Mama or Shernette unless I have to.

My life at home becomes more and more stressful with hate for Shernette, Mama, and Mr. Isaac, but life at school becomes more and more delightful with love for my friends and my new passion.

4
Fifteen, Crazy Fifteen

Writing love verses is my new passion. My classmates and I write love verses and share them with each other. It's a new ritual for us girls—mostly fifteen-year-olds—in third form. I'm pulled right into writing—the fun, the excitement, the words of love fill my head like what Jamaican rum and orange juice, chilled with ice do to the drinkers in the bars in Jamaica. They drink and talk and talk and drink and lose their minds. I write and read and write and read and fill my mind and soul. I don't think about what or how much I write or what this writing will do to me. I don't even think about Mama, what she'll say or do if she knows what I write. The love verses consume my life. I stay in class during my recess to collect, make-up, and write more love verses. It's not like I'm missing anything outside. I don't have money, anyway, so I can't buy food, and I don't want to trail behind one of my friends with money.

"Raquel!" I call her before she leaves the classroom. "Do you have any verse?"

"Yes." Raquel sits next to me. She's one my best friends. "Listen." Raquel recites.

I'll cross the ocean

18

> *I'll cross the sea*
> *I'll cross the river*
> *To bring you back to me*

"I just made up this one," I say.

> *Love does not hide*
> *Love stays by my side*
> *Love moves like a tide*
> *Love takes me on a ride*
> *Love makes me so, so, so wild*

"Yes, go on." Raquel laughs. "Sounds good. Let me write that one down."

"Raquel, I'm going to make my own love-verse book tonight. I'll show you on Monday. I'm going to write all the love verses I can think of in it."

"I'll read it when you bring it on Monday. How's Robert?"

"Alright. Still pestering me." I don't tell Raquel too much about what Robert and I do. I can't tell her about the hammers and nails. All Raquel knows is that Robert likes me and he won't stop bugging me to talk to him.

~~♦~~

My skinny legs and fast-walking stamina transport me in a short time from school to home. Mama is not home from work yet. I search one of Mama's handbags for needle and thread.

The love verses make me think that love can be beautiful.

My hands and mind can't wait to create this book. I dash to the dining-room table, rip some blank sheets from my notebook, fold them in half, cut the halves, fold them in half, and sew in the center of the halves.

I squiggle *Love Verses* at the top on the front cover and scribble my name at the bottom.

In my book, on each page, I pour all the love verses I have gathered and made up in class. I write new ones to fill the empty pages.

The "Songs of Solomon" in the Bible, reads:

> *Let him kiss me with the kisses of his mouth—*
> *for your love is more delightful than wine….*
> *My love, you're like a dove….*
> *Come, my lover, let us go to the countryside,*
> *let us spend the night in the villages.*
>
> *….*
>
> *There I will give you my love.*

My love verses are clear. I think better, too.

Mama will be home soon, and Shernette will leave the kitchen soon. I must finish the book before they come into the house. I stash *Love Verses* into my school bag and push my bag next to my bed.

After dinner, I shower, read some love verses, and fall asleep. Saturday morning, after breakfast, Shernette and I, without speaking, sweep, polish and shine the floor and cut the grass and rake the yard.

An hour ago, Mama left the house. I knock on Andrea's front door, not letting Shernette see. I show Andrea the *Love Verses* book. She likes the verses and laughs as she reads them. See, that's why I love Andrea. She knows how to have fun.

"I did that too, when I was younger," she says. "But I didn't make a little book like you."

"You did this too?"

"Of course. Almost all the girls swapped love verses."

"Wow!"

"Where are you going to move to?"

"Just around the corner. Water Lane. I'm going to live with Colin's aunt." Colin is Andrea's boyfriend or soon-to-be husband.

"That's not far. I'll come and see you when I buy ice."

"I'm going to miss you."

"Andrea, sorry to get you in trouble."

"No problem. We're sisters, right?"

"Yeah."

"I have to go, Andrea, before Mama comes back."

"See you. I'm going for a walk soon." Andrea closes her door.

I dash to play with Bridgette. I don't play with her much because she's too young for us to do the things I want to do. But I read with her sometimes. Now I have all day to read *Love Verses*. I take *Love Verses* from my bag and read and read. Then, instantly, I decide to go outside and play.

~~◆~~

"Come here!" Mama says. I don't like the tone of her voice. I sense trouble. I run to see what has made Mama into an even angrier devil.

I near the doorway and notice Mama. She stands as a warrior, shoulders high, chin thrust forward, one hand resting on her hip. The other hand clutches— no!—my precious *Love Verses*. I forgot to hide my book in my school bag before going outside to play. I freeze. Lord, please deliver me. I want to find an escape, anywhere—even if the earth takes me in, I don't care. I'd rather lie underground than stand on this ground and face Mama's wrath.

Mama's eyes bulge as if someone has replaced them with goggles. Her mouth opens. I think fire will come out. Before she utters a word, words fly from my own mouth.

"It's not mine. It belongs to Raquel. She wrote my name on it."

"Huh. Do you think I'm a fool?"

"No, Mama."

"Is this what I send you to school to do? To write about love?"

"No, Mama."

Mama flicks the cover of *Love Verses*, and the first love verse stares at her. Her body twitches and she glares at me. She reads:

> *Roses are red*
> *Violets are blue*
> *Sugar is sweet*
> *But not as sweet as you*

I stare at my bare feet for fear of my eyes meeting Mama's eyes.

"Uhnn. Who is sweeter than sugar?"

I dare not reply. I can't understand why Mama makes a big deal over *Roses are red*, when she sings the song almost every day, especially when she's washing clothes, as if Mr. Isaac is really sweeter than even brown sugar. I want to scream, to say, "What's wrong with *Roses are red*, and if you don't want me to write it or sing it, then you shouldn't sing it." I want to say, "There is no harm in writing love verses, and it's too bad for you that you didn't get to write them when you were fifteen."

Mama does not put away or return *Love Verses* to me. It's like she wants to torture me, to make me feel bad for writing. Mama flips several pages and gawks at a page in the middle of the book. Then she gawks at me, too.

"So tell me," Mama says, "since I don't know anything about the Minister of Education. When–did–you–talk–to–the–Minister–of–Education?"

I still refuse to answer her questions because I know she does not want answers. She wants to humiliate me. I'm sure she knows I can't answer this question, either. When I copied and wrote the verse about the minister of education, I thought it was funny. Now I like it better than all the other verses. Why can't she like it too? Why can't she laugh too?

"Uhn." Mama reads:

> *The minister of education*
> *Says that men's occupation*

She pauses. She has a right to because I can't even mention the words I wrote there in the next two sentences. So I'll skip over them. Mama continues:

> *To increase the population*
> *Of the younger generation*

I stand quietly as Shernette looks on, probably glad that I'm in trouble again. I don't understand why Mama has to read to me what I've written, why she has to read aloud what I have memorized, and why she has to read another verse as if I don't know them all.

> *Tulips in the garden*
> *Tulips in the park*
> *Two lips when two lovers meet in the dark.*

"Lord, what is becoming of this child?" Mama says. Her voice expresses scorn. She utters what I know is a big lie, a mutter about in her day she could have never done anything like this. I know, of course, that Mama couldn't have done anything like this at fifteen because she was not in school and she was not writing love verses.

"From now on," she says, "when you go to school, make sure you come straight home. No more activity after school. You have too much spare time on your hands. I can't believe you write this after all the church, Sunday school, and Bible school you go to. You have too much bad company. That Raquel. Don't let me see you talk to her again."

The place I enjoy, the after-school activities I'm so involved in, will be gone. Everything. I am caged.

I wonder what Mama would do if she knew I had asked George at school what sperm looked like. I wanted to know because our health teacher said boys get sperm. Anyway, after George told me that sperm looked like snot, I felt sick. Mama wouldn't have to worry because I don't ever, not in my life, want to see something like that.

I don't know how to enjoy my cage as I enjoyed after-school activities. I'm surely going to hell if I don't have a closer relationship with God.

5
I Surrender All

I'm a mixture of joy and pain, good and evil, child and adult, as I struggle to be good again.

Pastor Richard, the Deacon, and two members sit on the pulpit and face the congregation.

"Let's sing *I Surrender*," Pastor Richard says.

Members stand, some sing and some hum.

Church members sway as they always do when they sing. They tap their shoes and snap their fingers. Softly. Members march up and down the church's aisle. Some dance in circles, eyes closed, in the spirit, conquered by the Holy Ghost. Some raise their hands, fingers shaking in the air, eyes staring above, tears drifting down their faces, dripping off their chins. Members shout, "Hallelujah, gl-o-r-y be to God."

Pastor Richard uses his pleading voice, the voice that comes from his belly, from his soul, from all his deep Godly feelings. Pastor Richard uses the voice that gets everyone to cry, to jump, to dance, to feel the presence of God.

Pastor Richard's voice shudders in the microphone, louder than everyone's. "I surrender all. Will you surrender your life to God?" Pastor asks in his proper, speaking, preaching voice. "Repent to God? Will you?"

Tambourines jingle, shakers rattle, hands clap and voices boom, "Glory to God." "Praises to His name!" people in the congregation say.

Pastor whispers into the microphone, "Will you be kind and let him into your heart? He looks at the members. "He will not turn you away."

Members' voices hush to a sweet soft tune. Tambourines and shakers slow.

I feel the presence of God, and I want to give praise with more than my hands. I close my eyes and feel the words.

I hum. And I cry. And I sing.

I cry because I remember my life as a good Christian and I don't know what to do now and I love Jesus. I know it's not right, but I don't know how to stop the hatred inside me. I can't stop Robert from seeing me. *God! Help me.* I love Jesus. I do, I do. I clap softly to the beat, open my eyes and glance at pastor, who stares at me.

Tears escape.

"Come to the altar, Sister." Pastor Richard's face looks as if he carries the weight of my sins, my troubles. My troubled soul. "Let Him forgive you."

Pastor Richard speaks only to me. I know, I know, I know. He cares for me. Pastor sings, shakes his head, his hand still outstretched. It pulls me to him like a magnet. I must leave my seat, walk to him, and let him pray for me.

I wander from my seat to the altar and fall on my knees, bow and close my eyes.

Members shout, "Praise be to God. Thank you, God."

"Forgive me, God," I sob. "I'm a sinner. Forgive me."

Pastor Richard stands beside me. He plants one hand on my shoulder and the other on my head.

"Yes, ask Him to forgive your sins. Don't let anyone tempt you to live a life that's wrong."

I nod.

"Will you accept God into your life again?"

I nod.

"Thank you, God. How great Thou art." Pastor Richard twitches in the spirit, his hand lifts from my head and returns to the same spot. "Pray for Sister Peaches," Pastor Richard says to the members. "She needs your prayer. She wants to live a life that is right."

"Glory!" Sister Joanne shouts. "Glory be to God."

Live a life that's right, I tell myself. Tears stream down my cheeks because I know that I'm not as strong as before, and I know I need more than prayers. I need God by my side every hour, every minute, every second. I need Him to protect me.

I feel the members staring at me, their gaze of love, joy and triumph, and I worry even as I tell Pastor Richard that I'll accept God into my life again, because I did before, and it didn't work. It didn't work right after I walked home because Robert was there, waiting for me.

I wipe my face and open my eyes. Pastor Richard says, kindly and softly, that I can go back to my seat, and he reminds the members again to pray for me and my soul. They say, "Amen. Yes, we will. Bless her soul, Lord."

Pastor says the same before-church-dismisses-speech, the benediction. "May the grace of our Lord and Saviour Jesus Christ, remain and abide with us now and forevermore. Amen."

The members gather their Bibles and hymnbooks. I feel their love, their joy that I'm back. Some walk over to me and tell me that I have made a good decision. Some hug me and some smile at me, and some tell me they are proud of me. I smile and hug them back and I know that this journey back to God is hard for me.

Outside the church gate, I say to Raquel, "See you tomorrow."

"See you too," she says.

~~◆~~

I clutch my Bible and stroll into the dark along the side of the road to my home. *Live a life that's right.* I see Robert's silhouette at the side of the road. He calls my name and pulls my hand. I don't resist. Even if I try, he'll win. He's determined. I still remember the promise I just made to God and I want to tell him I'm a Christian now, and that I can't talk to him again. I cry inside, *Oh God, forgive for me doing this.*

"Rob… I'm…." I can't say what I have to say.

Robert tightens his grip.

"I want to become a Christian again."

"I know. I saw you at the altar."

~~◆~~

"Robert, Mama says we are doing bad things," I say.

"If you're going to take the blame," Robert says, "you must play the game."

"But."

"If you're going to take the blame, you must play the game. Don't take the blame if you won't play the game."

Whatever that means. Play the game and take the blame or don't play the game. What choice do I have?

~~♦~~

Church. Again.

The church members say I'm not holy any more. They say I'm still seeing Robert. They're right. They say I'm still a sinner. They say Raquel and I are backsliders. I sit on the backbench or the last bench at the back of the church. That's normally where the sinners sit.

I feel bad, unclean, sitting in the house of God.

Now I worry that Pastor Richard will get some kind of revelation from God about what I did with Robert. If he does, I'll be in big trouble. I worry that all the members will swarm me, dancing in the spirit, speaking in tongues, resting their hands on my unholy head, rebuking the devil from me, revealing my sin. Worst of all, I don't want God to strike me down to the church floor. I may never get up. I've seen members who've sinned, down on the floor, rolling, begging for forgiveness, mouths frothing saliva, as if they were dying. I felt bad for them.

I'm a sinner and I can't stop sinning. I can't take sitting on the backbench any more with the feeling that I'm the worst sinner, the stares as if sin—my sin—is printed on my face. I can't go back to church. I'll stay home and read whatever I can find, but not the Bible because I know I will feel afraid of God.

~~♦~~

Mama says I should get ready because the church members are coming to the house.

"They're going to have a prayer meeting for you."

I say nothing.

I can't believe this. Because I don't go to church, Mama's bringing the church to the house. They're coming to pray for me without my permission.

They can always pray, but I know they can't change the person I've become. Granny used to say, "You can take a horse to the well, but you can't force it to drink." I wish the members luck. I don't hate them because they don't really spread any gossip about me, but I hate the fact that they want me to stop doing what I can't help myself from doing. Robert won't let me go.

I dress and wait.

I pull back the curtain a little and peek through the window. What a sight to behold. I laugh to myself. The Christian posse. So holy looking? They're making a trip to my house as if I had asked them to— *Please, come and save my soul, please.* Pastor Richard and six women, with their hymnbooks and Bibles in hand, all my prayers go to them. I wish them all the luck in the world to save my soul.

Poor Mother Meg. We call her Mother because she's one of the older members. Mother Meg, strong in the spirit but weak in the flesh, hunches low, low to the ground, as if she's about to keel over on her face. Mother Meg's eighty-something-year-old legs wobble like sticks in water. Even with the support of her walking stick in one hand and Sister Marla holding the other, Mother Meg looks as if she can hardly move. I don't know why, with her unstable legs, she decided to make this trip with people with strong legs. The Christians file through the gate, into the yard and onto the veranda, leaving Sister Marla and Mother Meg behind.

I tiptoe from the window and, "as a lamb to the slaughter," as Granny used to say, I sit where Mama says I should sit—on a chair by the dining room table—and I wait. I cross my arms and cross my ankles. Shernette and Bridgette stand in one corner and make way for the Christians to roll in.

They all greet Mama, Bridgette, Shernette and me. I receive them with glances and nods. Some sit and some stand. I sit, lips sealed, head bowed, eyes staring into my lap, and arms folded across my waist. I listen to them and wish they would disappear.

Soon they sing. Sister Joanne bursts into shivers, her hands shooting up in the air. "Hallelujah. Bless her soul, Lord."

Pastor Richard prays softly, "Heavenly Father, here is your daughter. She has strayed, and oh God, please bring her back."

Mama says not a word, probably hoping that the people from church can get through to me, as she cannot.

"All we can do is to continue to pray for her," Pastor says. "She's not bad."

Sister Joanne used to love me very much. I don't know if she still does. Once, when Mama couldn't afford to send me on a school trip, Sister Joanne paid for me. I will never forget that. I used to say that when I get older and get a job, I would pay her back or do something nice for her. But, right now, I can't think about anything nice.

Sister Young blabs about my life not pleasing to God, and that if I get hit by a car and die, I should wonder where my soul would go.

I'm mad. I don't like anyone scaring me about death and hell. Scaring me won't work.

Hands grasping her cane, head nodding to every word others say, Mother Meg calls my name. I look at her. Shernette and I, out of the goodness of our hearts, used to clean Mother Meg's house on Saturdays. I don't do it any more, but Shernette still does.

"I'm old and soon to die," Mother Meg's voice trembles.

Yeah, yeah. I've heard her story over and over, about how long she's lived, and about how soon she'll die.

"Live a good life," Mother Meg continues. "Don't let no boy take over your head. Jesus loves you and I love you. You listening to me?"

I nod.

~~ ◆ ~~

It's "Reading Out" day. Since I don't go to church any more and because the Christians claim I'm a sinner, I'm expecting that they'll "read me out" or remove my name from the list of church members. I will not be a member of the church any more.

Of course, I don't attend the event. Who would want to show up for something like that? Despite my absence, the church members go about their holy business and remove the known sinners from the membership circle.

The news reaches me the next day.

I'm officially a sinner again. I guess I can behave like one. I can now wear shorts, pants, earrings, bangles, and sleeveless clothes. I'm free. Free to sin.

~~◆~~

"Since you are not in church and you don't go to church, make sure you stay home every night," Mama says.

What she said doesn't bother me. I can't go anywhere anyway. I'll have to stay home and read or find more ways to see people I can't see.

My life, it's like a pebble sliding down and down and down in an endless channel. I don't like the way Mama keeps looking at me.

"You don't want to go to church any more? You wait. I'm going to set you straight." Mama gives me the evil eye.

6
Late Last Night

Buying ice each evening is my duty. I buy ice to cool the lemonade I make to drink with dinner. Apart from school, buying ice is the only duty that lets me escape from my cage. I stop to see all the people Mama banned me from seeing: Andrea, since she doesn't live with us any more; and Raquel, because I can't see her after school any more. I see Robert at nights when I can, but not as often as I used to because of all the eyes and ears around me. I make my rounds today.

I have to move fast, but I use a trick. I walk calmly out the house with the ice bowl in my hand as if I'm not in a hurry. As soon as I know Mama or Shernette can't see me, I walk with speed. I dash up the lane to see Raquel, dash down the lane to see Andrea, and dash from the lane and into the shop to buy ice.

I think I stayed too long, gossiping with Raquel and her sister and blabbing with Andrea about the latest trouble in my life with Mama.

"Fifty cents ice, please," I blurt to the shopkeeper, and I hum as my legs shake. "Hurry up, please. Mama is waiting," I say to the shopkeeper.

"You just got here," the shopkeeper says and gives me a don't-rush-me-annoying glare. And I guess

34

I shouldn't have opened my big mouth because the shopkeeper now moves slower.

I slap the side of my leg. *Hurry. Hurry, please!*

The shopkeeper slowly turns around, slowly wanders to the big floor freezer, slowly hauls a big block of ice from it, slowly removes an ice chipper from a drawer, and—uh-oh. He quickly jabs and jabs the ice chipper into the ice until pieces fall away. I give the shopkeeper the fifty cents, give him the orange bowl, and he drops the ice into it.

I dart from the store and rush home. Near the gate, I slow my pace, wipe the traces of sweat from my forehead, and calmly walk into the yard as if I'm not in a hurry. I enter the yard and saunter into the kitchen.

Mama swings a gaze at me. Her eyes pop open, giving her evil eyes the opportunity to cast on me one of those before-death stares I see on angry people's faces in movies. "Um!" Mama grunts from deep down and puffs air from her nostrils and her mouth. Her face is like wrath.

"Why did you take so long to come back?" Her voice booms in my ears as a dog's angry bark.

"The shopkeeper took a long time to serve me." I lie.

"I don't believe you." Mama points her finger at my face.

I step back and say, "It's true."

"You didn't go somewhere else?" Mama pokes my forehead with her finger. "Even if you had to wait on the shopkeeper, you could never take so long to come back."

I stand still. I don't open my mouth.

"You know how long we've been waiting on you to bring the ice? The food is getting cold. Huh!"

I stare at the ice in the bowl.

"You are acting like a big woman. Like you make all the rules in here. If you don't listen you will feel," Mama says. "And when you feel you will learn."

I place the bowl of ice on the little table in the kitchen. Mama pours water on the ice chips to wash them and then drains the water. She dumps the ice into the jug of lemonade.

In silence, Mama, Shernette, Bridgette and I eat and drink, and Mama sighs and sighs. Forks jam into fish and clink on plates. We crunch food and gulp juice. The voiceless noise at the table and in the room doesn't feel right. Danger. Fear. The fear, like fire, burns in my stomach.

The wind flaps the curtain against the wall. Goosebumps rise on my arms in the heat. A loud wave slaps a rock and the waning echo lingers until it dies. Mama's eyes, hard and angry, stare out the window, then at her food, then at Shernette, who gazes at Bridgette, but not at me. I squirm, uneasy from the tension.

Mama finishes her dinner before we do. She trots from the table. Not a word.

"I'm finished," Bridgette says. "I don't want any more food."

"Eat some more," Shernette says.

I say nothing.

I wash the dishes, put them away, and take my shower.

Night comes.

Mama's not home, and it's almost nine. I haven't seen her since she walked away from the dinner table.

That's strange. She's usually home or she tells us where she will be if she's not meeting Mr. Isaac. I don't know what it is, but something is wrong.

I kneel in the middle of my bed and pray. It's been hard for me to pray since I left the church. What do I tell God? It's hard to pray when I feel I'm not living right in the sight of God. It's hard for me to pray when I feel that I'm a sinner and that the only thing I can say is, "God, please forgive my sins." It's hard to pray when I know I'm on the bus to hell. But I have to try tonight. I have to try to pray because I don't like the way Mama looked this evening and because my troubles are piling on top of each other like a growing hill.

I cry.

Dear God, please hear me. I want to ask you some questions. You said I should love and not hate. But how can I, when I feel sad all the time? How can I, when Mama makes me sad and I have to cry? When laughing is something I don't know how to do any more? When honoring my mother, as the Bible says, so that my days will be long on earth, is hard to do? Deliver me from the bad things that await me. Please God, help me to be good. Make me love you more. Help me please. Amen.

~~◆~~

"I heard you crying last night," Fraser, a neighbor, says as I walk from the house.

I look away from him, hold my head down, and wander to the toilet at the back of our yard.

I hate Mama more than I ever did before. I hate her with all my heart and soul. She's in the kitchen, and I can't stand to know she's even there.

37

I amble back to the house, shower, and think and think and think. I don't need to stay here.

My joints ache.

"Bad child!" I hear the voice, still in my head from last night.

My head aches.

"Bad child!"

My back aches.

"Bad child!"

I hurt.

"Aaahhh!"

Water stings.

Whoever says water, soap, and bruises go together? Foolish me. I better get out now. The water and the soap only sting me more.

I must do something. What? I can't remain here and play the silent, dead, daughter any more. Silence and anger can do only so much.

"Bad child!" Mama said as her hands swung back and forth last night.

And what did I do? Cry. "Ahhhhh!" No more crying here for me.

I tiptoe from the bathroom, hurriedly slip into my one-piece khaki school uniform, and scan around me because I don't want anyone to catch me.

Perfect.

No mother.

No sisters.

Good.

The way is clear.

Yes, I can take it now.

I'm not coming back.

7
Emergency Money

I sneak into Mama's room, reach behind her bedroom door, grab the old, gray, Sixties handbag that hangs on a nail and rummage through it. I glimpse the crisp Jamaican twenty-dollar bill Mama hid in a pocket. I check behind me. No one. I grip Mama's emergency savings and shove it into my pocket. It's now *my* emergency money, *my* bus fare—to flee from her. I dash out to walk to school.

The road leading to Happy Grove High School straightens along the big open field where boys and men play cricket and football. Patrick Patterson, a great Jamaican cricket player once played here. The road bends along the kindergarten. It dips by Clear Springs, the lonely stretch where no one lives except ghosts and where trees border one side, and the sea borders the other. The road rises just before a concrete sign:

Happy Grove High School
Founded by the Society of Friends (Quakers) in 1898.

A sharp left turn leads up the small hill to the primary school.

The road meets with another road that rises and rises, and like a tiny island, the proud Quaker Meeting House, with its big iron bell that rings when its members die and before Sunday morning services, towers over everything else. Around it, tombstones reveal stories of members, including Granny, who have passed on, and the green hill cascades to meet the road below. Several yards across from the Quaker Meeting House is Happy Grove High School, a few buildings scattered on the land. Metal mesh and barbed wire, along with a gate, cage the buildings—as Mama cages me.

I climb the road that leads to school. At school, I hide in the girls' washroom, afraid to let my friends see my eyes, red from crying. Around them, the skin have grown large, swollen and red from fingers rubbing and wiping the river of tears. As I cry silently, with tears still running, I hear Raquel. Her humming lifts me from the toilet seat. God must have sent her because I had hoped to see her. I run to meet her.

"Raquel."

She looks around at me. "What happen?"

"Mama beat me."

"For what?"

"I don't know. But I won't live with her any more."

"Where did she hit you?"

"Feel." I turn my back to Raquel.

Raquel slides one hand over the bumps on my back. "Geez. You bawl loud?"

"Of course."

"Oh my! Your mother did that?"

"I'm going to Kingston to find my father."

"What did she beat you with?"

"I don't know."

"Your Mother is wicked."

"Yes."

"What are you going to do?"

"Find my father."

"I'll come with you."

"Serious? For real? You'll come?"

"Of course."

This is the best news I have heard in a long time.

"Thank you, Raquel. I need your company."

"Yeah, we are going to Kingston."

"Look Raquel, I have enough money to pay our fares." I pull the twenty dollars from my pocket and show Raquel.

"Let me see." Raquel grabs the bill and studies the bill. "Where did you get it?"

"Don't worry."

"Yeah." Raquel waves the bill. "We are going to town."

"Give me before you lose it." I grasp the money and push it back into my pocket.

Raquel and I celebrate. We chat about the good life we'll live in Kingston. Raquel wants to enter the Jamaican beauty pageant. I want to be a singer. During the lunch break, Raquel sneaks from school with me. I buy lunch for her and me, and we amble to Stony Heaven on a paved road that surrounds one side of a big house on top of a big hill.

At Stony Heaven, the wind blows softly, the sun shines brightly, and the grass spreads neatly around the big house, a mansion first owned by some white Quakers, from the United States, who helped to build the Quaker high school and church after slavery. Like a lighthouse, one side of the house looks over the Quaker meetinghouse and Happy Grove High School, which, although on a hill, appears to sit in a valley. On another side, below the house, a forest stretches for about a quarter of a mile and leads to the mouth of the road. Below the trees, smaller houses stand aloof, separated by shrubs and zinc fences. Below the houses, where the main street snakes, sits the shop where we bought our lunch. Below the street, sea waves climb rocks and lick the shore.

Raquel and I rest in the shade under a large tree outside the gate and by the big house. We wait for the bus to arrive to take us to Kingston. Raquel's smooth, shiny caramel complexion and her hairless skin seem perfect for a beauty contestant.

"Squeeze this one," Raquel says as she touches a pimple on her forehead.

"Eww! That's a big one." I turn and touch Raquel's zit and as I turn, my eyes drift into the valley and rest on our school. I freeze.

"What's wrong?" Raquel asks.

"Too much."

"What!"

My heart pounds.

"Peaches, what!"

"They're watching us." I tremble. My mouth opens.

"Who?"

"Look." My hands shake as I move my fingers from Raquel's pimple and point to the horde of students and teachers who stand like a long, thick wall at our high school. "The whole school is watching us."

"Geez!" Raquel puts her hands on her head.

"They must have heard the news."

"Oh, no."

"Jesus!" I glance down the hill. "Raquel, we're in big, big trouble."

"What now?" Her voice quivers.

"They're coming for us."

Two women lumber toward us.

"Who?" says Raquel.

"Your mother and Robert's mother."

"What?"

"Run."

Raquel and I bolt. We have no plan, but we dash in the same direction, leaving our school bags and lunch garbage behind. We scramble into the yard and dash on the mat of grass. Then, I think we're going to die. I can't believe it: Dogs howling like a pack of hungry wolves, dogs surging around the corner of the house and zooming in on us. We scream. We spin back toward where we came from. My mind thinks only about the exit from this yard. I guess Raquel thinks the same, because we dart in the same direction. Twigs snap and leaves smash under our feet. We pant. We scream. One dog, too close to me. Gosh, I feel his breath at my heels. He's about to chomp on my feet, yank me to the ground, and rip me to pieces. Ahhhhh! I'm now through the gate. I escape with Raquel close behind me. Our bodies tremble. Our teeth clatter. Raquel races to her mother and I find myself beside Robert's mother. Terrified, Raquel and I glance at the dogs as they growl and growl, showing their long sharp fangs.

"Where do you think you're going?" Raquel's mother shouts.

"Nowhere," Raquel replies.

"You were going to run away?"

"No."

"Don't run away," Robert's mother says to me. "You can stay at my house if you want."

Wow, this is the first time Robert's mother has spoken to me. I usually say hello to her. That's all. I can't believe she's so kind.

"Thanks for the offer but I don't want to," I say.

"Well, go home. Go home to your mother. You don't need to run away."

"OK."

I don't know how Robert's and Raquel's mothers heard about our plan. But another student was in the washroom when Raquel decided to leave with me. She must have told. Thanks to nosy people, now I have to go to Kingston to find my father all by myself.

~~◆~~

The four of us walk back to Hector's River. Silently, Raquel and I linger behind the two women. Since Mama's house is first on the way back, I say goodbye. What's the consequence or my punishment for trying to run away? I can't imagine anything worse than last night, but I'm prepared for anything. Exhausted from the sun, the walking up and down the hill, the dog chase and, most of all, last night, I drag myself through the gate to the back door. Who is sitting on the bare concrete steps as if she knew I was making my grand return? Shernette. She sits like a guard in the middle of the doorway. Seeing me, like police in the middle of a street blocking traffic, Shernette quickly stretches her arms in opposite directions and clutches the wooden doorframe, blocking my entrance. I bite my bottom lip.

"Excuse me!" I say.

"No!"

"Let me pass."

"No! No! No! Mama said not to let you in the house! No!" Shernette spits out venomous words.

I take a deep breath. I sigh. A loud sigh.

"Let me pass!"

"No!"

I hate Shernette as much as I hate Mama. I hate her for ganging up on me with Mama. I stand two steps below, staring with my evil eyes at my evil sister. My anger rages.

Hit her. Hit her, a voice tells me.

I climb a step to get closer to Shernette and cast a serious stare at her. I fight to control myself from striking Shernette. If I slap my sister, I'll have to prepare my aching body for a fight.

Hit her. Hit her.

Shernette, sitting there, saying what she's saying, seals my fate, my instinct, and my decision that I do not belong here.

"Mama said not to let you in the house!"

There is no turning back now to try to fix anything. No thinking that this or that will make things better. I'll have to take care of myself. Do what I have to do. Now.

"Fine," I say in my softest, angriest voice.

I'll find somewhere for myself. After all, I'm fifteen. I hate Mama and Shernette for banning me from the house. I shake my head, grip my forehead, and leap from the step. I turn and give Shernette my evil-eye stare. I feel like crying but I'm not going to cry. I've cried too much since last night. They'll never see me again. Not ever again.

8
Please Stay

The sun blazes, but in a few hours, it will wander from the sky, day will meet night, and then I'll get to see Robert. Somehow. Nights give us safety when we meet. Nights protect us from gossip and peering eyes. I'm sure Robert knows what's going on. His mother must have told him. But he doesn't know I'm banned from my own home and that I still have to find my father. Before I meet Robert tonight, I will have to talk with Andrea: tell her everything that happened. I'll ask her to take me to Kingston. Andrea is always on my side. She won't say no. I know. When Mama accused me of doing stuff with Robert, Andrea defended me, told me that it was OK for me to have feelings of love. Andrea and Mama argued over me. Now they don't talk. Because of me.

Still in my school uniform that hangs over my knees, still carrying my brown backpack, I trudge toward Andrea's house, toward Water Lane, the stony dirt passage. When rain falls heavily, it beats on the dirt, digs into it, exposes the heads of stones, and leaves potholes.

Men in the village always sit on the low, curved wall. The wall where men talk man-talk and drink Red Stripe Beer and puff Craven A cigarette smoke. The wall where they recover from long workdays and talk about their encounters with women and brag about their children. The wall where they sit and watch little girls grow, where they make snake sounds to get my attention, where one man told me I was a good girl, where another man said I acted like an aristocrat, but that I was nothing. The wall where two years ago, a man said to me, "Ah waiting 'till you're ripe." I'm glad the men are not here now.

~~ ◆ ~~

Andrea stands in her yard and removes plastic pins from clothes hanging on the line. I run to her. I tell her what happened at Stony Heaven. I tell her what happened last night, how bad it was, how bad I felt. I show her my bruised skin. I show Andrea how Shernette squinted her evil eyes, clenched her teeth, while she spoke her harsh words, "Mama said not to let you in the house." I drop Shernette's evil expression and now I cry.

"Mama is wicked," Andrea says. Her eyes trace the tear tracks from my eyes to my chin.

"I can't live here any more," I say. "I want to leave Hector's River. Please, Andrea, can you to take me to Kingston to find Papa? Please!"

Andrea is mad at Mama, I know. Andrea squeezes her lips together and pats my back with one hand. She glances at the sky. What to do with me, Andrea must wonder.

Say yes, Andrea. Say you'll take me to Kingston, where I'll find Papa. Please God, let Andrea say yes.

Andrea stares back at me as though I have lost my mind. "I can't," she says.

I'm shocked. She can't do this. What am I going to do? "Please, Andrea."

"Are you crazy? Go back home. You're too young. There's no place for you in Kingston."

"Please. Please Andrea, if you don't take me, I'll still go."

With what I have just told Andrea and with the welts she's just seen, I don't understand why Andrea can't understand that I want to get away. Her eyes still, lock on me.

I can get her to agree. I droop my shoulders, suck in my cheeks, pout my lips, fold my arms, and stand silently. I will relax only when Andrea agrees.

Andrea shrugs her shoulders and walks away as if she doesn't care, removing clothes from the line. She throws the clothes over her shoulders, one on top of the other. Andrea walks in the house, stays for a little while, and walks back out without the clothes. She glances at me.

I stand, frozen, as my eyes rest on her. *Say yes, Andrea, please say yes.*

A little smile appears on Andrea's face—and her dimples set deep. She walks to me.

"OK, we'll take the early morning bus."

"Thank you! Thank you!" We hug and I smile and we hug and we jiggle.

I stay with Andrea inside the house she lives in with her husband, Colin, and wait impatiently for the sun to cool, for the shadows to spread over Hector's

River, so I will see Robert. I had sent him a message to meet me at night.

The night falls deeper and darker. I shake my legs and stare out the window. The wind wails and raps the window and wanes in the distance. Crickets sing and fireflies flash their lights, enjoying their night freedom.

~~♦~~

I walk to meet Robert in an open field. I recognize his silhouette, his big, curly, greasy hair that stays in place with Vaseline, his strides—how his body lifts and falls, his lean frame and his hands—as usual, one in his side pants pocket and one swinging to and fro by his side. He saunters to meet me in the dark.

What will Robert say or do when I tell him I'm leaving? I hear him beg me not to leave. I hear him tell me, again, that I shouldn't leave. I see Robert hugging me, telling me it's OK.

I walk up to him, and I know he knows something's wrong. Yes, his mother must have told him. Robert stands in the lane before me with his arms open to hug me.

"Not here, be careful," I say. "Maybe someone is watching," and Robert reaches for my hands and holds them and we drift into deeper darkness and I say, "I have—news for you," and he speaks, his voice anxious, "What?" and I say, "I'm leaving Hector's River," and he says, "What? Why?" and I say, "Mama beat me," and he says, "Beat you?" and I say "Yes." And Robert says, "Don't go. Please. But if you have to, before you leave, stay with me for the night. I might not see you again," and I say, "OK," and

Robert says, "Meet me later tonight." He hugs me. Tight. My head takes comfort against his skinny chest. I am relieved that he doesn't seem worried about me leaving so I say, "What time should I meet you?"

"Wait in the lane in about two hours. I'll meet you."

"Where are we going to stay?"

"I'll get a room."

~~ ◆ ~~

At about eight thirty, in the dark, Robert meets me in the lane near where Andrea lives. I wear Andrea's beige dress. Robert takes my brown bag that Andrea packed with clothes and underwear. He hangs the strap of the bag over his shoulder.

With the fear that Mama might see us or that she might learn about our secret plot, since "bushes have ears" in Hector's River, we walk cautiously, like fugitives, away from the main street, away from the bright lights and through a dark bushy passage. Our eyes scan the dark, our ears listen for voices, and our feet delicately tread on dry leaves.

~~ ◆ ~~

In the darkness of the small room Robert takes me to, this room that belongs to his family, I cry as I lie on the bed beside him. My back hurts from the welts from last night. If I tell Robert about the welts, he might ask to see them, and I don't want to show them to him. Tears spill all over the pillow that does not belong to me.

"Sorry," Robert hushes me. "Don't leave me."

51

"I have to." I stare at the dark ceiling. I wipe tears and fight the sadness that boils inside me. A part of me wants to snap at Robert and blame him for all my troubles. I want to say, "You are the cause of all this mess."

"Please, stay with me," Robert says. "You can live with my family."

"I can't. I can't stay in this village with Mama."

There is nothing to hope for. My joy is gone, wrinkled like a sun-scorched leaf. Memories of last night, bitter, won't leave my mind. I can't tell Mama how I feel. I have to respect and obey her. I must. Children should obey their parents, the Bible says. But I think the Bible also says something about parents, something like parents should not provoke their children. The only way I can continue to fight back in a respectful manner is to leave Mama.

"I can search for my father, find him, and live with him."

"You know where he lives?"

"No, but Andrea will help me to find him."

"Do you want me to come with you?"

"No."

I don't want any more troubles with Robert.

Soon I'll be free of Mama. The feeling of freedom floods me with a big fear: leaving home, fleeing to Kingston, to a place I don't know and a father I don't know.

As I lie on my side, a tear slips from one eye, then another from the other eye, and I can't stop crying. I try to stop the tears, but they flow like streams that meet. The tears from one eye glide over the bridge of my nose and blend the tears from the other eye and the stream runs into and over my ear and onto the pillow. Like a wounded pig, little grunts escape from my mouth. I shake.

Robert and I stride from the room and into the pre-dawn darkness. We can't let anyone see us.

9
I Can't Describe It

We have to hurry so we don't miss the early morning bus. We stride toward the old yellow post office that stands with its back before the sea, behind a concrete wall, beneath a streetlight and beside Bottom Church.

On weekends, the village grows another soul, a happy soul, a musical soul, an electrifying soul. I'm sure, as usual, some of the younger boys—teenagers and young men—will still play music—reggae and R & B that boom throughout the village. And they will DJ too—a kind of sing-talk over music. I don't like some of the DJ songs, though—the nasty stuff that men DJ about women. Some parents will still allow their little girls and boys to dance. The children will continue to dance with bodies stolen by the sweet melody of music, bubbling or gyrating their little behinds in ways I like to watch but in ways I think are vulgar in public. And no one, not a single person will complain, because it's fun, especially on Sunday evenings where everyone dresses up to feel good, to entertain, to show off, and teenaged girls will meet teenaged boys. People in the village will not complain about the loud music. Not even the Christian women walking to church through the crowd with Bibles in their hands will complain because playing music is public entertainment for the young people and for everyone. And neither Pastor Richard nor his members will complain about the music even when it drowns the singing, the testimonies, and the preaching in the church. I will miss all of this.

Robert will come here, to this post office, to pick up the letters I will write to him every day we are apart. We will write with wonderful words, words that tell of our worries or woes. Our letters will keep us always, always together.

~~◆~~

Andrea waits for us before the post office. She smiles as Robert and I walk toward her. Her small white teeth, as neat and as straight as perfect dentures, glow in the dark. One of her cheeks reveals a dimple. I love her dimples. Andrea's long black hair hangs over her shoulders and back. With her black handbag over her shoulder, black skirt hanging below her knees, brown sandals on her pretty feet—like a beautiful woman in a picture—Andrea stands with her hands by her side. "Don't worry," I say to myself.

A feeling of love so intense and so unfamiliar rushes into my heart as I see Andrea, waiting alone in the dark for me, her sister. I have never felt this love before, this flood of, maybe, love in my heart. I can't describe it. This feeling makes me think that something was missing before now. Something—. A lovely little link to a broken chain. We now connect the long-invisible link to our sisterly love. I don't know if I feel this way because I am dragging my sister into my misery or because I'm wearing her beige dress or because I might not see her again for a long time or because Andrea is the only family member that I have now. My sister. I don't know why. All I know is that I love Andrea more than I've ever loved her. She's my true sister.

I walk up to Andrea and hug her deeply in a hug that says, "Thanks. I love you."

Andrea hugs me back and I feel the warmth of her embrace that says, "I love you, too. Take care of yourself."

I scan Hector's River, the land that stands like a little mountain and acre by acre drops to meet the sea. Over the post office, coal-black and orange clouds hang motionless over the horizon. The belly of sky spreads deep, dense, and dark. Behind the post office, the sea wheezes like the breathing of a tired, sleeping woman—a long, soft, but heavy snore in the quiet of the night, as the village sleeps still and silent. Small white waves bubble and race tirelessly to the shore, where they end their journey. The sea waits to entertain the village's fishermen who sit and fish in the boats they carved from big trees.

Facing the post office stands the lonely community center, surrounded by the big, empty green field. During the days the field roars with laughter and shouts from children; quarrels between women and men; arguments among women; people meeting people; brays from donkeys; barks from dogs; *baa*, *baa* from goats; and sometimes the bang of bat against a ball when the cricket team competes with visitors or screams from boys playing soccer. Big and little houses, some wood and some concrete, face three sides of the field. Late evenings and nights, smoke rises from fires people light to repel big mosquitoes and tiny sandflies. The early morning air—not too cool and not too warm—blows gently and reminds me of the serene look on Andrea's face as we wait for the Kingston bus, and I have to wonder why I didn't see the coming of the beating, night before last.

~~◆~~

Robert and I look at each other as the bus engine bellows in the distance and the horn honks like a big trumpet, waking the village. The bus leans around the corner, pulling its body like a big caterpillar showing off its blue and yellow and green and red. Bananas, bundles of canes, bags of coconuts, mangoes, and other fruits, saddled to a steel rail on top, seem ready to roll off. The baggage man stands at the back door on the last of three steps and leans from the door with one arm stretched out. Black smoke spouts from the muffler, and the stench of diesel fuel fills my nostrils. For a moment, I feel sick. I don't like the smell of diesel.

Robert holds my hands and squeezes my fingers to say, "Good-bye."

The bus screeches to a stop where we stand.

"Hurry up," Andrea says.

The baggage man jumps from the step to allow Andrea and me to board.

I pick up my brown bag. I rush to the back door, hop up the steps leaving Andrea at the front, dash down the aisle, scoot to an empty seat where I slide my behind across the seat to the window to glimpse Robert before the bus crawls off. Robert stands and stares and I stare out the window at Robert. We smile sad smiles.

Andrea plops beside me and the baggage man slaps the side of the bus three times and says, "Driver, move it."

~~♦~~

The driver toots the horn and cranks the big engine that roars. The bus jerks and rumbles on the road with its load. In one spin of the tires, Robert disappears from before me, as the bus carries me from the countryside and away to Kingston, the capital of Jamaica. Kingston, the place I know nothing about. Looking back, I see Robert's silhouette, shrinking. Then the bus winds around a corner and Robert vanishes.

My eyes dry with my constant glare out the bus window as the bus bumps over potholes and stops to receive more people.

Andrea, my precious sister, true to me as a mirror—whatever she says, she does—sits beside me. I must break the silence.

"We're going to see Papa?" I ask.

"Yes. But we will first meet John. So he can take us to see Papa."

I'll get to live with Papa, the father I long for. I want my father to hold my hand. My weary eyes refuse to stay open any longer. I place my head on Andrea's lap. Softly and hypnotically, Andrea strokes my hair and my tired eyes close to sleep, to shut away all my worries and fears.

The bus lurches to a stop at the crowded bus terminal at Parade in downtown Kingston. Parade seems too busy, too crowded, like my mind with thoughts bumping into each other, thoughts worried about thoughts, thoughts interrupting thoughts. *I'll see my father. Andrea will go back. Will Papa love me?* The passengers pour from the bus and scatter. I feel a little nervous, a bit strange. Sick.

"I feel sick, Andrea," I say.

"Cause of the bus ride?"

"I don't know." I inhale and exhale. The sick feeling diminishes. "I'm feeling a little better."

"Good," Andrea says.

Andrea hooks my elbow with hers. We walk among a pack of people.

On the street, children in different uniforms, with braided hair and ponytails, some with ribbons, scurry to their schools. People hurry to work. Cars, bikes, vans, and buses push through the crowded street. A man, the conductor of a mini-van, shouts and motions us toward his van. Dollar bills pile between his fingers. The end of a red, green, and gold belt, Rastafarian colors, dangles from a buckle down the front of his pants, and a gold rope chain circles his neck.

Andrea and I scurry toward the mini-van. The conductor, glad to load his van with passengers, smiles at us. A gold front tooth glitters.

"Seat at the back, fill up the back," he says.

I squeeze to the back with Andrea and rest my head against her arm. Andrea stays quiet. Her mind seems far away. Even though the van is full, the conductor still charms people to ride, still tries to stuff in more people so he can make more money, I know. Listen to him.

"Spanish Town Road, Spanish Town Road. Lady, come on in, you looking nice. Brethren come on in."

Everyone, I guess, wants to get to wherever they are going soon because they still pile into the van one by one, and some, with no place to sit, crouch over other passengers who sit in the seats. The van speeds off.

"Stop here," Andrea shouts.

Andrea and I squeeze between people. She pays the conductor and we hop from the mini-van and walk to see John.

~~ ◆ ~~

John looks a little surprised seeing Andrea and me walking up to him. We hug our brother as we meet him. Andrea spills the news of what happened and why we're in Kingston. John seems to have mixed feelings on the situation saying, "If that's what happened, then maybe she has a right to want to leave." He also says, "Well, why she has to leave?" I remain quiet. Andrea pulls John away and they and talk. I wait. I think John did the best thing by coming to work in Kingston. He found Papa. I'll find Papa, too. I wonder what they're saying.

~~ ◆ ~~

The three of us hop on a J.O.S. bus. Anxious to get off, I think the bus moves too slowly. I wonder how my father looks. For some reason, a sharp image of Papa did not stay with me, only a faded picture of his face. I remember the bronze color of his skin, like John's, his spiraled hair, the way he looked when

Mama left him. Will he like me? Does he care about me? My hair, brushed back in a ponytail, hangs down my back. I want to look good when Papa sees me.

I dream of Papa. He recognizes me and I am happy. He runs to meet me in slow motion, like *The Six Million Dollar Man* on television, and his arms open to receive me. He kisses my forehead, stares at me, and brushes my hair back. He says, "I'm so glad to see you," and I say, "I'm glad to see you, too."

"Next stop we're getting off," John whispers to Andrea, who wakes me from my dream. John rings the bell, and the bus slows and stops.

We trek to a place with an unpaved passage with red soil and stone, and wood-built houses—shacks— with raw-unpainted wood.

"People don't buy this land," John says.

"Where they get it from?" I say.

"It's nobody's land or government land," Andrea says.

"The people are squatters," John says.

"What's a squatter?" I inquire.

"They don't have the right to live there," Andrea says.

"But nobody troubles them," John says.

"You're coming to see your father?" a woman says to John.

"Yes," John says.

"You father went to Montego Bay," the woman says.

My throat tightens. I feel the vibration of my fast, pounding heart. I stare at the ground. Tears fall on my shoes.

"You know when he'll come back?" John asks.

My ears open up to hear good news.

"No," the woman says. "I don't know. He didn't say when he'll be back."

The red dirt and the stones seem to mold together, forming a dark cave around me. My feet feel pasted to the ground.

"No. No." I cry with my hands over my mouth, muffling my cries. My tears sprinkle the parched red dirt. I hunch my shoulders, fold my arms across my chest, and sob.

David's prayer in the book of Psalms, pops into my head.

> ...do not leave me nor forsake me, O God of my salvation
>
> When my father and my mother forsake me, then the Lord will take care of me....
>
> Wait on the Lord; be of good courage, and He shall strengthen your heart....

I don't know why this scripture comes to me, but it seems right because I believe that my mother and father have forsaken me. And I feel that I need the Lord to take care of me and strengthen my heart.

"Your father went to Montego Bay," remains in my mind. Andrea clutches my arms, and I march like a silent, wounded soldier on my journey back to the bus stop, feeling the painful rhythm of my heavy feet as though I wear iron shackles on my ankles. I don't have a mother and a father. What will happen to me now?

10
The Tears Didn't Stop

The shock of not seeing Papa hurts. But I don't know why, why on earth I thought he'd be right where I wanted him to be, like I had lost something that I expected to find anywhere, even in a place I had not lost it. And yes, I wish my father were a tree I planted. Knowing it would always be there. In the same spot.

Will I ever touch him and hold his hand again?

"You father went to Montego Bay."

All I have now are John and Andrea. Soon even they might turn against me. Andrea is too nice to tell me when I'm wrong. Maybe it was wrong to leave Hector's River. John is always a pleaser, too kind to say no. Papa was kind, too, but alcohol made him unkind. My sister Rose said that. I shall not search for Papa any more. I shall not, even if at times he pops in my head, I shall not. I shall not think of him any more.

~~ ♦ ~~

The question that needs an answer now—where do I stay? I cannot ask. Words right now are like scared birds in a cage with an open door, wanting to come out but afraid, scared they might fly the wrong way. So I wait again for my dear sister to bail me out, to use words for me. Knowing I can rely on her, Andrea speaks for me again. But not the words I want to hear.

"So, maybe you should come back home," she says.

"No. I can't. Please understand," I say and look at her. "Help me to find another place. Please."

"Where?" John asks impatiently, as though he's frustrated.

"Andrea," I say, "all the students and everyone were staring at me yesterday. I can't face them. I can't go back. The whole village must be talking about me."

"Let me think," Andrea scratches her head and looks at me.

"I don't have any place for you to stay. I only have one room," John says. John lives in a room, in a house that belongs to Aunt Betty, my father's sister. I don't remember how she looks.

"Maybe Aunt Betty will let her stay there," Andrea says.

"No," John says. "She won't. The house is already full."

"Let's go back to Parade. Mrs. Chan sells in the market. She might take you in."

Mrs. Chan is the grandmother of Steve, Andrea's ex-boyfriend, the father of Andrea's son, Owen. Andrea and Steve met when Andrea lived in Kingston and that's how she had Owen who now lives with Steve and his grandparents. When Andrea decided to leave Steve for reasons I don't know, Steve was angry.

He punched and slapped Andrea and they wrestled as Owen and I watched and cried. I felt much sadness for my sister. So young, so pretty, so energetic, so beaten up. But that was then. A few years ago. I think Steve will be nice to me.

"OK. I'll go back to work and the two of you can go," John says.

Andrea and I saunter from the bus, cross the road, walk toward the marketplace. People on the street sell food, from fried fish to fresh fruits. Everywhere I walk, a new aroma meets me. Afternoon nears, so we buy lunch. We munch on spicy beef patties, gulp down pineapple drinks, and walk up to the booth where Mrs. Chan sells tin measuring cups and shiny tin lamps.

Mrs. Chan recognizes Andrea. She stands up, and she and Andrea do a long-time-since-I've-seen-you hug. They greet each other with, "How are you," "Not too bad," "I'm good," "You look good, too," greetings and make-you-feel-good talks.

I stare at them with their smiles, happy to see each other.

"Cute sister," Mrs. Chan says, and I smile.

Now the hugs and smiles are over, and the serious story waits to be told. Although this meeting is because of me, I leave it to Andrea to tell the story. She tells it. How lucky I am to have her speak for me.

After their talk, Andrea turns to me and says, "You can stay with Mrs. Chan."

"Thank you," I say to them.

"I'll take you there, and you will see Mrs. Chan when she gets home. We'll get to see Owen."

"Thank you," I say again to Mrs. Chan. "Thanks for taking me in."

Andrea travels with me to Trench Town, where Mrs. Chan lives. "Two years ago, during the 1979 election, many people there died," Andrea explains. "That was the bloodiest election Jamaica ever suffered." Andrea also says that I might hear gunshots at night.

Trench Town, or at least the street where Mrs. Chan lives, is a real "Concrete Jungle," as Bob Marley sang. The road, the sidewalk, and the house where I will stay are concrete except a tiny patch of dirt in the yard, I guess to plant flowers. Behind the house, the land has red dirt and patches of green and brown grass. Not far from the Chans' house, on one side of Spanish Town Road, lies May Pen Cemetery. This land, which the government purchased in 1851, thirteen years after slavery officially ended, sprawls with concrete tombs big and small filled with the bodies of people—children, adults, the rich and the poor.

Andrea introduces me to Mr. Chan, and I meet Steve again. Owen runs to meet Andrea, who hugs him tightly. Then Andrea takes me to a house where two of Steve's cousins live. The cousins say I'm cute. I smile. They say I look like Andrea. I smile. Andrea tells them I'll be staying with Mrs. Chan. They tell Andrea stories about the recent election and the shootings. They point to a nearby house and talk about a man who heard a knock and opened the door and a gunman shot the man who opened the door in front of his family. They say the dead man's son wants to be a cop when he grows up so he can find the killer and put him in jail. The son also wants to get all the bad guys off the street so they won't kill again.

Back at the Chans' house, Andrea says she has to leave. Tears run from her eyes like an overflowing dam as she hugs Owen goodbye and says goodbye to me. The tears don't stop, even as I try to console her.

"It's OK," I say.

Andrea and I hug, kiss, and wave goodbye.

~~◆~~

Tonight, like last night, I'm in a room that does not belong to me. I sleep beside Owen. I cry. Night in this place is a haunting silence, shattered by the bang-bang of gunshots. I guess I will have to start getting used to it. I know that Jesus, in a glittering gold-framed picture, will protect me. The low-ceiling, windowless room, cooling off from the hot day, feels like a warm oven. No more crickets chirping, no more waves splashing against rocks, no more roosters crowing at dawn. Maybe all I will get here are the sounds of gunshots. This is my choice. I cry until I fall asleep.

Before I rise, a big bang, iron against iron on the iron bars that cage us in the house, wakes everyone except for Mrs. Chan. She already stands in the small kitchen, dressed for work. Something—a little voice—something deep down tells me something is wrong.

11
Let me Die!

I jump from the bed, and dash behind Mrs. Chan, who walks through the shadowy hallway to the front door. She squints and folds her lips together. I stay close behind her.

My thoughts race like a thousand wild horses. Mrs. Chan turns the key that seems too slow, too loud, too much for me to bear what I must face. The key clicks, and Mrs. Chan turns the handle. Light blinds my eyes. Mrs. Chan opens the door more, and light floods the living room.

As light pours in the doorway, Andrea stands outside the iron bars that cage the front of the house.

"What happened?" I say.

"Mama called the police on me. The police warned me that I must bring you back or else they'll throw me in jail and put you in reformatory."

Jail for Andrea. Reformatory for me. Or go back. I search for words but can't find any.

"Come in," Mrs. Chan says.

"You have to come home, Peaches. I don't want to go to jail."

"No," I cry. "No. I'm not going back. Why won't she leave me alone? I don't want to go back."

"You have to come," Andrea pleads. "I can't go to jail for this."

Mrs. Chan unlocks the iron lock with a key.

"I don't want to live with Mama. Why does she want me back? I don't want to go."

"Please."

"No, no," I cry.

~ ~ ◆ ~ ~

The bus drives slowly back to Hector's River. Andrea sits with her hands in her lap, and I stare out the window. Why am I going back to a place I no longer feel I belong, a place where days and nights will run marathons, a place where I should laugh but instead will cry? What if I don't go back? Will my mother make the police throw Andrea in jail and throw me in a place where bad children stay? Andrea is scared of jail, and I am terrified of juvenile reformatory and any kind of beating or whipping.

When I went to work with Mama, before I started elementary school, Mama told me many stories. She said she was often whipped. Teachers whipped Mama. Granny told Mama's teachers they could whip her however they wanted, "but just save her eyes."

Mama was whipped for plotting to run away from the woman Granny left her with. She wanted to run away when the woman made Mama lick her pee from the floor. Mama peed there because she was afraid to go outside and pee in the dark. I guess running away runs in the family.

Mama finally moved back home and her older brother whipped her. Mama said she was not far from home when her brother caught her with her boyfriend and "he beat me all the way home." Mama didn't run away. Mama said she walked, bravely, not flinching—taking all the beating. Before she turned sixteen, Mama was out and on her own. She found work as a domestic worker in Kingston.

Usually, when Mama tried to beat me during the day, I would run and run. I would run away and stay away from Mama until I knew she had forgotten and lost the anger to strap me any more. One day, I ran away after I had I peed the bed. Mama had walked into the room one morning. She felt the bed I lay on and patted my clothes to see if I was wet. I was. I prepared my behind for the three or four-wake-up-slaps Mama gave. Mama slapped my behind and muttered, "I'm getting tired of this big child peeing the bed. Get up!"

I sleepily rose out of bed. Mama reached behind the door for the big, brown, broad leather strap. I backed away, closer to the open back door. A wave splashed against a rock. I ran through the door, hopped down the seven steps, sprinted to the wire fence, crawled under, trespassed through Mr. Harry's land, jumped over a gutter, scampered over a field, walked behind some rocks, inched underneath some grape vines and let the grape vines and the rocks hide me.

I knelt on a little patch of green grass surrounded by two little rocks. Around me grape vines spread over the rocky earth. I'd been to this place many times before; been here to pick grapes and to use the big broad, fan-shaped grape leaves to fan myself when I was hot.

That day, I did not want grapes or grape leaves. I cried. I looked to the big open sky above the vines, even though I could not see it. The sea stood about seven yards from where I knelt. Waves thundered and crashed on the rocks. Waves roared and rolled on the shore. Ocean spray settled on me.

I prayed and I cried. "Lord, take my life. I don't want to live any more. Lord, why do you make this happen to me? Why me? Help me! Help me! I wanna die! I wanna die!" I pounded and pounded on the grass. "Let me die!" I screamed. "Let me die!"

Another wave splashed against a rock. Ocean spray settled on me again. I wanted to jump over the cliff and into the sea as a voice in my head said, "Jump, jump."

I could not. I could not do it. I prayed and I cried. Hours passed.

The sun sank into the sky. Shadows from the rocks and grapevines concealed me. I was afraid. I had heard that ghosts dwelled in the bushes at night and they liked to swing on the grape vines. I was afraid. I didn't want to open my eyes. I didn't want to see a ghost. I wanted to go home. Yet, I didn't want to go home. I couldn't go anywhere else in a raggedy, pee-smelling nightgown. To hide from the ghosts, I pulled my knees up to my chest and curled my upper body into my legs. I covered my face with my hands. That was how I decided I would sleep through the night – until I heard talking. I raised myself from the little patch of grass, rested on my knees and peeped through the vines and the leaves.

Mama and Shernette were searching for me. They called my name.

"Yes," I answered.

I crawled under the vines and between the rocks. My joints ached. I stood and walked to Mama. I was thirsty. I was hungry.

I still peed the bed after that day, but Mama did not hit me any more. Then one day, I realized I did not pee the bed any more. Mama did not wake me and feel the bed any more. I didn't remember exactly when I stopped. I didn't remember how I stopped.

That was the last time Mama tried to beat me until two nights ago, the beating came without warning.

I don't understand why parents beat their children, and I don't understand why I may have to go to reformatory. I've heard bad things about it. Adults say it is like jail. I guess I'm really bad. I will go to Mama's jail instead of reformatory.

And this time, as the bus nears Hector's River, I know for sure, the punishment will be more severe than before. I don't know if that's better than reformatory.

I'll have to face everyone, all the eyes from the villagers and the yak-yak-yak from the spies and gossipers. My classmates will talk and that's one reason why I'm not going back to that high school in that village.

~~ ◆ ~~

At Hector's River, the bus stops before Mama's house.

"Go to your mother," Andrea says in a sarcastic tone. "Go—on."

I remember Granny's words, "You can take a horse to the well, but you can't force him to drink." Although Mama forces me to live in her house, she cannot force me to love her. My mind will still be free.

Andrea hisses, frowns, and folds her arms as she stands before the gate and waits for me to turn and walk down to Mama's house. I don't know what to say to Andrea because I don't know if I will ever see her again or if I'll be able to talk to her again.

"She can't split us, Andrea." My voice cracks.

"I know," she shakes her head.

I feel like I can't breathe, that feeling, the one I always get when I'm angry. I feel as though a big lump rests inside my throat, like I'm choking on something. My head jittery, my hands shaking, more tears coming. I try to restrain them.

"Go," Andrea says again, softly.

Before I step toward the house, an excited voice across the street shouts, "Peaches!"

I didn't expect anyone to see me coming back. I had hoped to go secretly to Mama's house. I turn and let my eyes travel across the street and rest upon the person who yelled out my name. Oh, Gosh. Grinning and thrilled to see me, stands Pam. And I now know the news of my return will reach Raquel faster than a telegram. It's not that I don't want Raquel to know I'm back, it's that my escape wasn't successful and I am ashamed.

'Did you see Paul and Elijah up in Heaven when you and Raquel went up there?" Pam shouts.

"Wish I did," I say and fake a grin. I want to run. Why does Pam want to remind me of Stony Heaven when Raquel and I ran from the dogs?

"I ask Raquel the same thing, but she said she never saw a soul," Pam says and laughs.

I cannot describe the experience of running from big dogs at Stony Heaven. I wish a whirlwind had snatched me as it snatched Elijah. The only wind I felt was the wind against my face. It was a miracle I escaped. Pam will never understand.

"I have to go."

"All right," Pam says.

The door is shut but unlocked. Mama. She's not here. Neither is Shernette or Bridgette. Shernette will call me a thief or captured bandit when we fight, I'm sure. Weary and sweaty, I let myself fall face down on my bed. What will Mama do to me?

12
Female Has Just Escaped

One. Two. Three. Three weeks drift by.

My hatred for Mama digs deep into my mind like tree roots deep into soil, filtering the air, increasing my desire to escape. Every day I watch the sun appear. Every day I watch the sun disappear. Every day I wait for yet another day. Every day I pray. I pray in my mind, in a whisper. I pray for my life, pray that God will release me from this cage. I pray that I'm not pregnant. *Dear God, please protect me.*

Silence is my friend. As the weeks pass, I get more and more used to saying the same words without feeling guilty. Necessary words. I still have to respect Mama, but I don't have to say anything else.

My everyday greeting words:

Good morning.

Good afternoon.

Good evening.

Good night.

My polite words with the pause in between—because I don't really want to say the word Mama:

Yes, Mama.
No, Mama.
I don't know, Mama.
My words of gratitude:
Thank you.
Thanks.
No, thanks.

~~ ◆ ~~

I am stubborn, more stubborn than I imagined. I am a rock anchored in the sea. Like a wave, Mama washes and crashes over me, trying to shake or move me. But I'm a rock in a turbulent sea.

I wonder if she knows how much I hate her. I can't tell her. She probably would wring my neck. She probably thinks that I'm mad at her. She can't stand it—I know—she can't stand my stubborn silence.

Deviously, cautiously, under the shadow of my face, I cast my eyes at her movements. Every now and then, when I know she isn't watching, I glimpse her. I see the way she wants to slap me into talking, the look in her eyes as though she wants to whip me again.

I notice the controlled rage in her movements like when she jerks the scarf from her head. She twitches her head, frowns or curls her lips and knits her brows. How does she get her skin to pull together like that?

~~ ◆ ~~

Today Mama's woman friend visits the house, and they talk about me. They talk loudly, whisper, talk loudly again and laugh more loudly.

"She's bad."

"She has a man."

"I'm ashamed of her."

And I have to sit. Yes. I have to sit and listen to them talking about me as though I do not exist or as though I am the worst girl in the whole world. I sit in my room, listen, and pretend I don't exist. I can't allow words to bother me. Mama's words. Any words.

"The child don't have any manners," Mama says. "I should send her to reformatory. It will set her straight. She is nothing that I expected her to be."

Expected? I'm not supposed to exist, but I have to react to this? Expect. I don't know why she has expectations of me. I wasn't even expected to be in this world. Just an accident. She told me that her friend saved me. But she said she was glad I was here. Maybe she regrets her decision now. I feel angry and sad when she talks about me to her friends and when she allows them to talk badly about me.

"Disgusting behavior," the woman mutters.

What is disgusting for sure is hearing two big people talking about me as if I'm invisible. That's disgusting.

At the dinner table Mr. Isaac chews a chicken leg. "The child is bad," Mr. Isaac says.

Shut your mouth and chew your food, I say in my mind. Worry about it going down your throat and get off my case.

~~◆~~

Mama cooks for him every day. He comes to eat and then he leaves. He gives Mama money to buy food.

"Uhn," Mama says, "she's rude."

I want to shout and say, "Talk, talk. Talk as much as you want because I don't care," even though I'd be telling a lie. I keep my chatter inside my head.

~~ ◆ ~~

I throw my anger at my little sister, Bridgette. She will not talk back or tell on me. I tell her to disappear from me sometimes.

For eight years, until Bridgette decided to make her entrance into this world, I was the youngest. Now Bridgette walks up to me and stares at me. I stare back and make sure no one else is around. I open my eyes as wide as I can and I stick my tongue out to scare her away. She doesn't move. She still stares at me and I slap my hand with another hand and point at her to tell her I will slap her. "Scram," I say. My voice low and firm, my eyes like a witch, I only need to say one word to chase Bridgette away. I don't need her sympathy, I need freedom. She's now the same age I was when she was born. In a few months she will be nine.

Bridgette heard the beating, I know. I don't know if she saw. I don't know what else she knows, but she knows all that is wrong in this house, I'm sure. She knows that I'm not happy, that I'm evil and I'm living in my own evil kingdom. But she remembers not to get too close to me. She moves quietly around me. She loves me, I think. But as long as I live in this house I will not have a place in my heart to give or receive love. Yesterday I said, "Vamoose" to Bridgette. I gave her my evil eyes. She backed away quickly, and I laughed silently at my evil self. But last week I helped with her homework because she would not go away.

Bridgette is learning. She bothers me less. Like Mama and Shernette, Bridgette passes me today as if I'm invisible. I enjoy being invisible because I don't have to talk to anyone. Shernette and Mama, well, I'm staying far.

The days drift by meaninglessly, and I'm feeling meaner. I have reasons to feel this way. I can't see Andrea, Raquel, and Robert.

I'm glad the school year is almost finished, but it's bad that I have to see some of the students pass my house. I don't want to go to school to feel eyes burning my body or listen to tongues thrashing me.

~~◆~~

I dream of running away. Again.

But I can't.

Juvenile reformatory waits for me. I heard the kids there are evil. Though I'm evil, I want to stay away from other evil children. Evil is contagious. Evil grows, and once it grows, it's hard to control. You can't chop it down like a tree and hope that the roots will rot and vanish. It's like bamboo: If you chop everything you see, but miss the roots, it pops up again in the same and new places. Evil kids become evil adults. Dear Lord, bless my evil mind and my soul.

I have no hope of ever escaping, since the stupid police will hunt me down like a crook on the loose. I don't know who they'll get to bring me back to this prison or reformatory if I attempt an escape. Certainly not Andrea. Mama told them I was fifteen, told them

I was a runaway, and told them that Andrea helped me to escape. I'm sure she didn't tell them Shernette barred me from entering the house. I'm sure she didn't tell them that she whipped me. I dream of escape. I would like to escape, but I don't want to hear this radio announcement:

Fifteen-year-old female has just escaped. She stands five feet six inches. Weighs about 110 pounds. Has a straight nose. Small, evil eyes. Massive jawbones, according to an unnamed source. Normal ears. Fingers long enough to play guitar or piano.

She has a scar on her forehead, but sometimes she covers it with her long hair, which she usually combs back in a ponytail. Medium-brown complexion. Not so bad looking.

She has pimples, mainly on her forehead. Also some brown spots, a result of her picking the pimples. The pimples are not contagious. But, according to another unnamed source, she has been quarantined at home – after her escape.

We don't know the reason for her escape. What we do know is that this is her second escape. She may have an accomplice. It might be more difficult to catch her a second time. This teenager, according to her Mama and her former

*friends, is cunning and evil, with strong
hatred in her heart.*

*Do not approach her. Call the police if
you see her. She could kill.*

I smile and think of other running-away stories.

~~ ◆ ~~

Three weeks pass. The silence is poisonous. Mama
and I cannot tolerate it any more. I'm dying. Mama's
dying. And for sure, she has to stop it. "I can't take it
any more," she tells her sister. "Maybe I should send
her back."

I can hardly keep myself from letting out a big
sigh or even jumping in the air. Mama might send me
back? I close my eyes, smile, and throw my fisted
hands in the air. I can't let Mama know that I heard
her words.

~~ ◆ ~~

Two days later, I am sitting at the dining room table,
gazing out the window, seeing another day die.
Mama—I don't like that name any more—walks into
the room. She stands behind me.

"Go," she says.

OK, this is my imagination. In my desire to flee, I
imagine too much. My silence finally renders me
insane. I am talking to myself. I'm hearing things. But
the sound did not come from me. If "Go" did not
come from me, then I need to hear it again to
confirm that it was not my own voice. I turn around

and look up at Mama, look in the eyes that shot me for three weeks. Those eyes show defeat.

"Go," Mama says in a softer voice. "You can go. It's better for you to be happy somewhere else than sad here."

All I know is that there's a jubilee inside my head but I can't show it. All the knots are now unknotting inside me. Should I bolt from the house before Mama changes her mind or wait and pack my clothes? For a long time I have not heard her speak like that. Since I became her nightmare, her voice has been cold, strong. I don't know if I should jump for joy or scream or run.

If I pack, will she think I'm presumptuous? I stare at her, my eyes asking what to do.

"You can pack your things," she says, "in the brown bag."

"Thanks." The word moves from my mouth like breath.

Mama wants the poison to leave the house.

Since I cannot fit everything in the brown bag, I choose some skirts and t-shirts, two frocks for church, in case I decide to go back, a red and blue pair of shorts, and underwear.

I don't know where I am going in Kingston, definitely not Montego Bay, not hunting down any father any more. Anywhere and anything in Kingston is better than here in Hector's River. I won't have to cry any more.

I take light steps from the house, hoping Mama won't change her mind. "Thanks and bye," I say. I wave with a stiff hand. I don't know why I'm feeling a little sad for Mama, because I'm evil and I'm not supposed to because of what she did that night. I'm not supposed to care about her. Maybe I'm not so evil. Mama, Shernette, and Bridgette stand at the door. They stand still.

I walk from Mama's house under the endless, enchanting evening sky. I'm free. I stare at the round rock by the sea where I once hid when I drenched the bed and where I walked with the wind against my skin. I'm free. But where, exactly, do I go?

PART TWO
NOMAD

13
Send Her Back Home

It's early July, and school is out. I ride the bus alone. In Kingston, I feel too ashamed to go back to Mrs. Chan's house. Instead, I follow Andrea's directions to Aunt Betty's house, the house where John lives.

John and Aunt Betty are at work, but I meet her two youngest children: Christine, one year older than I am, and Victor, younger. He looks around ten or eleven. Maybe twelve. I don't know. He doesn't say much as he watches cartoons on television. I also meet two girls, daughters of my father's brother who died—don't ask how because I don't know—and Aunt Betty took the girls in. They are younger than I am too. I bond with Joanne, the bigger girl, in an instant. I wonder if it's because neither of us has a father. Joanne wants me to stay at the house. Christine is friendly. I don't tell anyone why I left Mama. I tell them that I want to live in Kingston like John.

Aunt Betty arrives home. She has the same complexion as Papa and the same kind of hair. She looks as if she was pretty when she was younger.

"Hi," Aunt Betty says to me in a way that is not inviting. With the big brown bag in my hand, I know she knows I'm in trouble – or I am trouble.

"Aunt Betty, can I live here with you?"

"No," Aunt Betty says. "Your brother lives here already."

I hold back tears.

What now? I walk to Joanne, and as I tell her what Aunt Betty said, I cry.

"Don't cry," she says. "Cole is nice. You know our big cousin Cole, right?"

"Yeah," I say. "I listen to his songs on the radio."

Joanne gives me Cole's address and directions to his place. I tell everyone goodbye, walk to the bus stop and board the bus.

I arrive at Cole's, and who's here? Aunt Betty. She stares at me. A man with an Afro sits on the veranda and talks to her. I know he's Cole, the singer. He smiles with me. I say, "Good afternoon."

"Aunt Betty, how did you get here so fast?"

Aunt Betty smiles but does not answer. Maybe she took a cab or got a ride.

"Go inside and sit down," Cole says. "I'll talk to you soon."

In the room next to the veranda, I sit. I don't have a good feeling about Aunt Betty.

"Don't take her in. Send her back home. You have no place for her," Aunt Betty says to her son Cole, the nephew of my father. I sit and listen to them, cry, and wipe my tears.

"Goodbye," Aunt Betty smiles at me as she leaves to go home.

"Goodbye," I say to Aunt Betty and pretend I did not hear what she said to her son. I want to call her a witch or Aunty Evil, but instead I smile, a smile so hard to smile.

"You can stay here," says big, tall Cole. I love him for that. I love him because he is part of my father. Cole will shelter me. Cole will feed me. I know he cares for me. I am now a part of Cole's family.

How can Cole be so good to me? How can his mother be so bad to want me to leave when they are of the same blood? My mother—well, how can I hate my—mother? I am her blood. But it happens. People are different, I guess.

~~◆~~

This white house on Chancely Street is my new home, my salvation from Mama, Shernette, and the spies in Hector's River. Cole's girlfriend, Sally, and his two children, a twelve-year-old girl named Sarah and a ten-year-old boy called Ray, live here, too. Sarah, who has a body bigger than mine, speaks softly and likes to be quiet. She's nice to me. She lets me sleep beside her on her double bed. I sleep in the corner or by the wall. Ray smiles a lot and has his own room.

Sally is not Sarah or Ray's mother. I don't know why Sarah and Ray don't live with their mother. I don't ask. Beautiful, adorable children. I love Sarah's pleasant look and tender smile.

The summer break is almost over. I won't go to school because I don't want to ask Cole for money for a uniform or bus fare. Mama taught me not to beg. There's not much to do in this house.

I stay here almost all day and watch television. I'm making up for the years that I barely watched television at my neighbor's house in Hector's River.

My period still hasn't come, but the television takes my mind from thinking too much about being pregnant.

~~ ◆ ~~

Staying alone in the house with Sally is like being a convict before a judge. Just when I think the questions will stop, she asks more. She tries to learn everything about me, to make me feel guilty, to make me confess.

"Did you go to school?" Sally asks me while I watch *Different Strokes*. I turn to her, and her face almost touches mine.

I want to say, *Of course, I went to school. I went to Hector's River Primary School. My grade-six teacher selected me to enter the national spelling bee, but later changed her mind and selected my friend.* Mama had bragged about me to a neighbor. I even finished grade six, and out of forty students, I earned the eighth-highest grade. After grade six, I went to first form at Happy Grove High School. My first form report was good. I got some A's and B's. My second form report was not as good as the first. My third form report was bad. I did not care about school any more. I did not finish third form. I came to Kingston. But it doesn't matter. The fact is that I went to school. But I will not tell Sally that I went to high school. I'll let her think what she wants about me. Why waste my precious words and destroy my voice talking to her? The less she knows about me, the better. If I tell her more, she will want to know more, and if I tell her more, I will later find out that I have told her things I don't want her to know. Talk little, I say to myself.

"Yes, I did. I went to school," I say to Sally.

"Can you read? Can you read good? I bet you can't."

"Yes, I can read."

I want to pop my eyes out at Sally and say in a sarcastic voice, *I can read much better than you.* Instead, since I don't want to be rude to her, I say again, "Yes. I can read."

I don't tell Sally that I read almost all the books in the small public library next to Happy Grove High School. It was summer break. I was eleven, and there was a book-reading contest. Inside the library, pasted before the checkout desk, a sign announced a summer reading contest. The person who read the most books would win one hundred dollars.

I wanted to win. I walked to the library every morning from Monday to Friday. I selected big books and little books, books about animals, about people, on riddles, on rhymes. I read books in the library and took books home. I didn't really want to read all the books. The ones I did not like, I read just the words on the pages, not for meaning. Reading for meaning was not part of the contest. I wanted to get the money so I could give it to Mama for my school uniform and food. Mama bragged to her friends that I liked to read. The more she bragged, the more I read. I recorded the number of books I read with the librarian each day. At the end of the summer, I ran to the library to claim my prize. I was sure that no one else read as many books as I did. At the library, I stood before the librarian. I wanted to say that I was there to claim my prize, but I didn't want to be so bold.

"I would like to know if I won the contest," I said to the librarian.

"Sorry," the librarian says, "Diane won. You read more books, but she read some good books and some were more difficult." I could not believe it. Diane, a principal's daughter from a neighboring village, won even though I had read more books.

Sally thinks only bad thoughts about me. I watch her grinning.

"Well, if you can read, prove it to me," Sally says. "I'll get a book." Sally walks from the living room.

I look around the living room at the television, a stereo, many LP records, and beauty and gossip magazines. Sometimes I read the magazines to know what's going on in Hollywood. The way Sally looks at me when I read the magazines, it's as if she's thinking that I'm looking at the pictures.

Sally walks back with *Alice in Wonderland*. She smiles. I smile back and wonder why Sally thinks I can't read *Alice in Wonderland?* I have read it so many times. I read it before the reading contest, and I even read it again this summer. I like *Alice*. I know the story so well.

Sally gives me the book. "Start here," she says.

I look at the familiar words, smile, and read aloud. I read one page and look at Sally to let her say stop.

"Go on. Read on," she says.

I read another page, stop, look at Sally again, and smile.

"More," she says again. "Read until I tell you to stop." I read two more pages.

"Ok," Sally says, "you can read a little." I smirk and give her back *Alice in Wonderland*.

One evening Sally asks, "Why are you here? Did your mother send you here?"

"No," I say, not wanting to talk about why I left Hector's River. I hope Sally doesn't know my secret.

"I bet I know why you are here," she says and bobs her head like a puppy. "I know, I know."

What does she know? I didn't tell her. I didn't tell Cole. All I told him was that I didn't want to live with Mama any more and that I wanted to live with my father. He didn't pry, didn't ask anything else. So I wish Sally would shut up, leave me alone and disappear or, better, die in some corner somewhere. With that look on her face and the way she says, "I bet I know why," she's taunting me, telling me she knows my secret. Why does she ask if she knows? That's stupid. Why does she bother me? Like some sweet pleasure to her—a taste of sugar in insipid water, she watches the questioning expression form on my face as I tense and my jaws tighten—Sally enjoys all of this.

"You ran away. I know." Sally's eyes open wide and wild.

I cringe. What else does she know? Maybe she's guessing what secret I hold within.

"You're not a saint."

I didn't tell her I was Saint Peter or Saint Paul or Saint Mary, so I don't know why she says saint. I don't pretend to be a saint.

"Drive your mother crazy, right? What are you going to do with your life? This is not a paradise, you know."

I hate her for questioning me. For taunting me. She should be happy to have me here. Another addition to the family.

"Answer me," Sally says. "Did you run away?"

"I didn't run away."

"But you're here."

"I took the bus. I didn't run."

"That's still running away."

"I didn't run away."

I don't have to admit to her what I did. It's none of her business what I do. This house does not belong to her, and I don't have to answer any more of her stupid questions. This house belongs to Cole, and Cole is my cousin. Sally is like a nail on a chair that pricks me each time I sit.

Look at her. All dressed up again, dressed like she's in the beauty parlor where she works, dressing other people's hair. She does this dress-up, make-up, nice-wife act every day as she waits for Cole to come home. She waits like a beauty contestant in a pageant, knowing she's already picked. Look at her, sitting on that couch, her legs crossed with her bright, mischievous eyes surrounded by eyelashes long and thick with mascara. Face powder covers her almost flawless brown face, and bright red lipstick paints her not-so-big lips. Her curled hair shines, and she wears perfume I hate. Gosh, I don't like the smell. Too much perfume makes me sick.

The sound of Cole's car nears the house. Sally looks at her clothes and pats her hair. With her mouth closed, she wipes her tongue across her top teeth. The car pulls into the driveway, and she grabs a magazine and listens and waits. Never before have I seen a woman waiting for her man like that.

Cole opens the car door and it slams shut. He pokes his big head through the open door. Sally, facing him, smiles a smile so big that nearly shows all her thirty-two teeth. She closes the magazine and tosses it on the couch to make him see that she was reading. She eases from the couch and walks toward him. I wish she would bump her toe and fall, but she does not. Sally meets Cole at the door as he shuts it. They hug. His big, strong, long arms surround her in a hug that I know only someone who loves someone a lot could give. Every day, when I get married, will I do that with my husband?

14
Tell the Judge the Truth

Evening settles. I walk to the bathroom for my shower. I carry my daily before-shower to-do list in my head. Go to the bathroom, close the door, lock it, close the window over the garage so no one will see my naked body, and pull the shower curtain to make sure I'm safe. Check the bathtub, wash the bathtub if it's dirty, take off my clothes, and take my shower.

One night, a night I'll never forget, something happened to me. Why do bad things happen at night? After that night I started my before-shower list. I wanted to make sure I was safe, especially before undressing.

It was dark inside my room that night. But it wasn't supposed to be dark. Mama wasn't home. I was twelve, I think. I try not to remember it. My bedroom window was broken. Many times Mama had begged the landlady to fix the window. She never fixed it.

That night, as I slept, a man climbed through my bedroom window. He must have blown out the dimmed lamplight.

The man lay naked beside me. I did not know he was there until I felt his hand moving below my waist. I woke up, opened my eyes and darkness shrouded my view of his face. Confused, I asked myself, one question after another, "Who is this?" "What do I do?" The more questions I asked, the more confused I felt. I didn't know what to do. I felt scared. I grunted. A low muffled cry escaped from my mouth.

"Shhhhhh." He placed his finger over my mouth. "Shhhhhh," he said again.

He moved his hand from my mouth.

"Who – are – you?" I said softly.

"Shhhhhh," the man said again.

I saw the shape of his face in the dark room. I lay still and circled his face with my nervous fingers. I wanted to know who he was. My fingers bumpily traced his thick moustache and his bushy beard. He placed one of his legs over mine. I felt more scared. Then, he crawled on top of me. I panicked more. I shivered from fear.

With his skinny legs, the man forced apart my tiny, glued legs. He squeezed his legs between mine. His fingers, rough, fumbled.

"Nooo," I cried softly. "Noo. Please. Please"

"Shhhhhh," the man whispered. He moved his hand and covered my mouth.

I could hardly breathe. I didn't know what he would do if I cried more. So I lay. Quiet. *God, please help me.*

Then I felt something.

"Mama!" I shouted. But she wasn't home.

Like thunder, the word burst from my mouth. Like lightning, the man sprang from the bed, bent, picked up something, maybe his clothes, and shot like a bullet through my door and then through the back door that he must have left open.

Andrea and Shernette raced to my room after the man left. They saw the open back door.

I lay on the bed, finally realizing that he was gone. I crawled off the bed and walked to the back door with Andrea and Shernette. The man had disappeared in the bushes leading to the sea.

"Help! Help!" Shernette and Andrea screamed.

The neighbors poured from their houses and gathered into the laneway beside our house. They crowded me. I told them the man must be One-One, a man who was new to Hector's River because I felt his face and I saw the shape of it. I told them he used only one hand. The neighbors suggested what I should say when I report the incident to the police.

Months later, at the trial, my knees trembled and my teeth clattered as the judge asked my name. He asked if I knew the man who came to my room. The big courtroom felt haunted. Everything, from the mahogany benches to the ceiling fans, appeared gigantic. Silence filled the courtroom. I was scared.

The judge asked if I saw the man in my room.

The neighbors' voices played in my mind:

"Tell the police that it's One-One."

"It could be Bob."

Mama's words played:

"Tell the judge the truth."

I took a deep breath and looked at the judge. I told the judge I didn't know who entered my room. I didn't want the man to go to jail if he wasn't the one in my room.

After the incident, I was scared to sleep alone. I covered my head at night.

Maybe it's not because of that man that I am so careful here in Cole's house. Maybe I'm just like that. Maybe I like to be private, like to go through my before-shower list. It's probably just a habit.

In the bathroom, I stretch over the face basin and close the window. I pull the shower curtain to one end and—Sally, behind the shower curtain, pops before me as her fingers come at me.

"Woof," she lets out a big bark.

"Ahhhh! Ahhhh! Ahhhh!" I scream.

Sally stands in the tub and laughs like a crazy woman in a horror movie, her big white teeth shining like axes, her big white eyes staring like a panther facing its prey. My heart stops for a moment, then beats like drumsticks pounding hard and fast.

All Sally says is, "I wanted to scare you."

Scare me? She did. With her head tilted to one side and her lips away from her big teeth, she grins like a clown. I think she must be a stupid clown, because I don't like this joke or whatever she thinks it is. Scare. I wonder if that is all she wanted to do.

I force a laugh back at her to prove I'm not shocked.

She points her index and middle fingers at me, grins again, and says, "I got you." Sally springs from the tub like a cheetah. I move out of her way. She laughs and laughs. I chuckle with fear. Her laughs echo in the bathroom and fade as she gallops out the door. I close and lock it.

The sun sets early today. The sky darkens to a dark-gray. I almost forget that the sun goes down over Chancely Street because the place is usually bright. The wind blows cool, fresh, and light. It's probably going to rain tonight or early in the morning. Clouds drift slowly and heavily.

One month has passed so fast since I moved into this house. I'm getting used to living here, getting used to Sally, getting used to her madness. I must be the only one who thinks she's mad because Cole loves her, or that's what he pretends. Sarah doesn't say anything bad about her, and Ray is so young and in his own world.

Cole is not here this evening. The house seems even darker when he's not around. He left two days ago. He's probably on a singing tour with his band, *Mighty Singers*.

I don't like talking to Sally—the same predictable talk—too many stupid questions about me, about Hector's River, about anything that makes me sad or upset. "So your mother left your father in Kingston to go live in the country with all the kids and now you're back?" Sally reminds me of Hector's River and Mama each time, when all I want to do is forget.

"Please, God," I pray. "Shut Sally's mouth today and forever. Shut it, please. For my sake."

Does Sally talk to Cole like that? Does she ask him many stupid questions? Does he answer her? Cole usually sings or plays music when he's home, but I don't know what they talk about in secret. Does she ask him why I'm here or does she tell him to make me leave?

"Kids, it's time for bed," Sally tells Sarah and Ray at 9 p.m. because school has begun. The two rise from the couch, say goodnight to Sally and walk to their rooms. I tell Sally good night, too. I can't stand to hear her loud, chirpy, annoying voice. I don't want to spend another moment with *Miss Interrogator* in the living room. Can't she tell that I want her to leave me alone? Maybe I should tell her to read my mind. She probably won't understand. She'll probably think I am giving her more clues about my past. I could make up excuses, say that I don't want to talk, that I'm not feeling well. Would she leave me alone?

I meet Sarah in the bedroom. "Sarah, you're going to sleep *now*, now?"

"Yeah. I don't want to be tired in the morning."

"Good night," she says to me. "And turn off the light since you're the last one in bed."

"All right," I say and push down the light switch. The room darkens and I crawl over Sarah to my corner of the bed. I lie with my back next to Sarah's back. We sleep.

In the silence of the night I hear Sarah: "Auntie Sally, p-le-a-se," Sarah says. "Please, s-stop." Muffled words. "Please, don't kill me Auntie Sally."

I open my eyes and there, Sally sits on top of Sarah. Sally's knees bend like a frog's at Sarah's sides. Sally's two hands and her bony, witchy fingers squeeze Sarah's neck. Sarah's head rises and falls and rises and falls back on the bed we share. She wants to talk but cannot.

I shut my eyes, my legs stiffen with my toes curled tightly, and my fingers clutch in fists close to my legs and my curled lips touch the inside of my clamped-down teeth. I better say a prayer. One last prayer before I die—God, not this way. I need to atone for my sins.

Dear God, don't let her kill me next. Please, dear God. Forgive me for all my sins before I die and let me go to Heaven. Forgive me. Amen.

I wait to die.

I peek. My eyes almost closed. Sarah lies silently. Sally, who is not wrapping Sarah's neck any more, looks at her hands. I shield my face as I wait for my turn. Sarah must be dead because I don't hear her any more and Sally sits on top of her.

The bed shakes. I peek again through half-opened eyes and see Sally's shadow slip from the room.

"OK, Sarah?" I push my face next to her ears.

"Uh," is all that Sarah says.

I close my eyes again. Sarah shuffles and turns on her side to me, her face to me. I turn to the wall as I did before, and stick my face closer into the side of the wall. I don't know how long I will have to wait for sleep to come. But I will continue to close my eyes.

Sleep comes to me long after Sally has slithered away. In the morning, Sarah naively asks in a soft voice, "Auntie Sally, what were you doing last night?"

I cringe. I look down at the slice of bread on my plate and listen, pretending I did not hear. I don't want Sally to come for me tonight. Knowing my luck, I might not survive. It might turn out worse than it did for Sarah. Whatever caused Sally to sit on Sarah in the middle of the night in a dark room, or whatever caused her to want to choke the life out of Sarah, is none of my business. I wish I could disappear from the table right now. I'll continue to sleep on my belly so when she comes in for me, she will be sitting on my back and not on my belly. I don't want her to squeeze out my intestines.

"Ha, ha," Crazy Sally laughs, showing those big white teeth. Her teeth don't look like teeth. They look like little axes, because she seems to want to hurt. Those teeth are for biting human flesh. Her hands are for strangling. "I was playing with you." The laughter in her voice sounds like the cackle of a witch in a book for children.

"Oh. I was wondering," Sarah says.

I bite on the bread and chew it with my mouth closed. It was hard enough for me to see it. Now I have to hear about it again.

"You were scared?" Sally asks.

"No. Not really," Sarah laughs.

Without raising my head, I shoot my eyes at Sarah, who sits beside me. Liar, I thought, lying that you were not scared. I eat the last piece of my boiled egg, drink the last drip of tea, chew on the last bite of bread and say, "Excuse me," and walk from the table, leaving the attempted murderer step-mother and her almost-murdered stepdaughter to continue to their crazy pretend talk. I walk to the bedroom and sigh. It's going to get worse living here with Sally, I just know it. It's going to get worse.

15
Canadian Shorts

Standing by the record player where music plays, Cole reaches for the rack of records and removes one. Cole and Sally play reggae songs or love songs some Saturday mornings and the sound, the rhythm, and the lyrics of the songs always devour every other sound in the house. The sound vibrates and digs into my ears, the rhythm crawls into my body, and the lyrics jump from my mouth and makes me forget all the bad things in my life.

This Saturday morning, after living with Cole and his family for over six weeks, I dress the bed where I slept and dust furniture—my Saturday morning chores. Then, under a soft soothing shower of water, I sing the songs Cole plays in the living room. And the thought comes to me to wear the shorts I love, my short red shorts with blue stripes at the sides with my white t-shirt.

Julia, my friend who went to live in Canada, had sent me the shorts. The shorts were red when I got them—and tight. Too tight. But I didn't want to give them away because I can't afford to buy another one and I've never had a pair of shorts like these—soft and silky. So I had put my dressmaker skills to work, opened the seams at both sides, and sewed a blue cloth into the red. Now I have my red and blue Canadian and Jamaican shorts.

I walk to the living room and sit on the couch.

"Nice shorts," Cole says. He looks at me sitting on the couch. His eyes drift from my head down to my feet. He smiles. Cole's smile reminds me of cool, bright sunny days. Not like today where darkness from the day darkens the house as the sun dodges behind clouds, sneaks out, hides again and returns—I don't know how long it will hide before it resurrects, red and ripe and ragingly hot over this house on Chancely Street.

"I got them from Canada," I say and smile back at Cole.

Lately I like wearing shorts. For years, I couldn't. Wearing shorts went against the rules of Bottom Church in Hector's River. Since I don't go to church any more, I wear shorts—not on the street—but inside the house.

"Canadian shorts? Nice."

"Come here," Cole murmurs. He holds a record in his hand.

The stereo blasts as I rise and stroll to Cole and stand next to him.

"A new record, is it?" I ask.

"No."

"Looks new."

"Sally is gone for the weekend."

"Sarah and Ray are with their Mom."

"I know. They told me they were going for the weekend."

"You like this?" Cole massages my shoulder with one hand.

"I donno," I say. My body tenses.

"Wanna dance?"

"No." I giggle. "I can't dance."

"I bet you can dance." Cole holds my stiff hand.

"No—truly. I can't. I don't want to dance."

"Want to sit over there?" Cole points to the couch I just came from.

"I don't know."

Cole directs me to the couch. I stagger backwards. Cole's eyes dart from my eyes to my lips to my neck to my chest and up again. I grin.

Cole caresses me. "Do you like this?"

"I don't know." I stare at the ceiling then at my feet and then into Cole's face.

"Sit," Cole says.

"I don't want to." I stand, afraid to sit. Cole gently wraps his arms around me with his body close to mine, not like how he hugged me before—not so tight.

"Sit, come on, sit."

"I-I."

Cole gently pushes me until my knees bend and my behind rests on the couch. He sits on my small legs. A faint, frightful feeling creeps in me. *This is not right.* Cole—what is he thinking? I fear to hear what he will say if I say no. With his face next to mine, Cole breathes stale ganja or marijuana breath over my face and I feel bad because I'm not supposed to feel good. Not this way with Cole because he has a girlfriend and he's been like a father to me.

"No. No. No!" My voice grows louder with each no.

"Cole, no," I mutter.

"Yes," Cole mumbles.

"No, Cole. I don't want to. Please."

Cole pulls me closer to him. He tugs my t-shirt up. I tug it down. Cole's eyes narrow with anger.

"You walking 'bout the house with your fat ass like you think I don't have feelings," Cole shrieks. He breathes like a runner. His two legs box mine together. Cole brings his face close to mine. His weight on my legs pins me and he squeezes my jaws and shoves his tongue in my mouth.

I squirm. And push. I turn my face away.

"No, please, no, Cole, " I mutter, close my eyes, push him and feel my legs lighten as Cole lifts himself from me as the music fades and dies and fearful silence looms in the house. I open my eyes. Cole towers before me. Two large wrinkles stand between his narrowed, red eyes that pierce into me.

"S-sorry," I whisper.

Swiftly, like the swing of a bat, Cole's hand flies toward my face and my eyelids lock tightly and his hand lands like a plank against my jaw and teeth bite into flesh that bleeds the blood I swallow. From closed eyes, I see darkness and little specks of light that shimmer. I cringe. Hot tears burst and slide down my face. With my back to Cole, I curl on my side on the couch and bury my face into the soft seat and cover the back of my head and my ears with my hands. I wait and wait for the next blow. I sob.

"Get out," Cole booms. "Out of my house. Get out now!"

I push my legs from the couch and hunch with my back to Cole. I glimpse his shadow. I stumble into the bedroom. I search for my clothes. I push my legs into the waist of a skirt and pull it over my shorts. I cry and tears drip on the clothes as I pack them into bags. Snot runs from my nose that I wipe onto the sleeve of my white t-shirt.

Mama's words play into my head. *"If you don't listen you will feel and when you feel you will learn."* I didn't listen to her.

With two plastic bags in my hand and my brown bag slung over my shoulder, I unlock the front door and scurry from the house and onto the street. I look ahead and down—down at the road. I'm sure Cole peers out the window at me. I'm sure and I feel if I look at the window, I will see Cole, so I keep my head straight on the road and walk until I think he cannot see me from any window in his house.

Saturday afternoon. The sun's heat penetrates my head where pain grips, jams and thuds. I stop. Sweat gathers around the plastic bags in my hand. I rest the bags on the sidewalk and press my palms gently on the sides of my face. My jaw stings at my touch.

I wipe my face and stop at a house where one of my cousins works as a domestic worker. I don't tell her the whole story, but I ask if I could stay with her. She says no.

I wander on the street until Chancely Street ends and meets with Oakley Boulevard, where cars, bikes, and vans flash by and women walk with umbrellas and men walk with hands in their pockets. I wait for a space in the traffic. Which way to take the bus? I will take it to the bus terminal and then think where to go next.

I cross the street and walk into a bus stop where a man stands and smokes a cigarette. The smoke rises slowly in the haze. I rest the two plastic bags on the ground. I ease the brown bag with the strap from my shoulder and rest it beside the other bags. I inhale cigarette smoke with a big sigh. My head still hurts and my jaw is tender.

I have no money. I want to ask Smoker for money. Though I have stolen money, I have never begged money and I need money to take the bus. How many ways can I beg money? Maybe I should smile with Smoker and wait for a while. No, I'll ask him now before the bus comes. "Good afternoon, sir," I say to Smoker with my shy voice and big smile and a heart that pounds fast. "Please, can you help me with my fare? I don't have any money."

Smoker hands me five dollars with some change. The bill smells like his cigarette.

"Thank you," I say. "Thank you very much."

My fare to the bus terminal is only fifty cents.

"No problem," he says.

I take the money and push the five-dollar bill in the side pocket of the bag with the shoulder strap. A bus rumbles toward us. Tires beat on the road. Brakes screech and the bus stops before us.

With his thumb and index fingers, Smoker clamps on the fire end of the cigarette. He drops the butt on the ground and stamps on it. Smoker motions me with his hand to go first. I pick up the bags, walk up the steps, pay my fare and walk to an empty seat. I sit at the window and rest my bags on the seat beside me. I put them there because I don't want Smoker to sit beside me. It's not that I don't appreciate the money from Smoker, it's because I'm in no mood to talk now.

Thoughts roam in my head as I stare out the open bus window. I think about Cole. I don't want to cry. I think about what happened in Granny's house nine years ago. Mama had left me with Granny. I was six. Frank was big and tall. He was older. Fifteen, maybe more. He was my cousin too. I didn't tell anyone.

It was dark. Early night. I sat on the veranda while Granny lay on her bed next to the veranda. Frank called me. Said he had something for me. A lollipop. I followed him to get the lollipop. He took me the backroom.

Frank lifted me and sat me on a table. He stood before me. He gave me the lollipop.

He used his hands. I asked him what he was doing. He said he was playing. He said I shouldn't tell anyone because he gave me a lollipop. Frank lifted me from the table and he walked out the back door and into the night. Burning, I walked back to the veranda with the lollipop. Granny snored. I waited for Mama to come home.

My two cousins, one on my mother's side and one on my father's side. Why?

Now I have to find a new place to live. I will find a home. I will find a family who cares. I will go to school. I will. I know God will help me to find a home.

16
Tracks of Welts Spread All Over

The heat from the afternoon sun surrenders to a cool breeze that floods the air over Parade. My face, the bruise and the sting enjoy the breeze. Squints of eyes on people's faces from the bright sunshine disappear. Pedestrians crowd the sidewalk and the road. I paw my way with my free hand, touching shoulders, brushing faces and sweeping against cotton shirts. Reggae songs blast, hagglers beckon and scrawny goats and mangy dogs sniff at crumbs on the ground.

Should I take the bus and go back to Hector's River or stay here in Kingston? Country or town? For country, I'll need more than five dollars to pay my bus fare. That's one reason not to go back. The other—I need to sit and think.

I walk to a shady area of Parade. I sit at one end of a long bench, knee over knee, hand under my chin, I lean back on the bench. I rest my bags beside me on the bench. People pass me. They don't look real. They appear as objects in space. They drift in the space of this park.

Two choices. Stay in Kingston or go back to Hector's River.

Two choices. I don't have a place to live here but I don't want to go back from where I came or to what I came from. Everyone in Hector's River must know by now why I'm not there. Some will say I ran away even though Mama sent me back. Some will talk about me, some will laugh at me and some might call me Runaway.

People in Hector's River give names to people based on how they look, how they talk and what they do. They named the boy with the darkest skin, Blackie. They named the boy with the big head, Cow Head. They named a woman with long neck, Long Neck. John named me Spoiled Fish because I cried a lot and Rose named me Nosy Parker because I was really inquisitive. I know inside that the people in Hector's River have already named me Runaway.

I can't go back. I can't go back to what I left. Yet my mind drags me there always and reminds me about things. Life. Like what happened the night that caused me to leave Hector's River. Whenever I remember that night, I cry. I feel the tears gathering in my eyes. I try to hold them back. I take a deep breath and swallow to switch my thoughts, to stop the tears, to stop this old feeling, the feeling and the remembering of the night that haunts me, the night that caused me to be here.

I don't want to cry in this public park, in Parade, in downtown Kingston. Parade, where British troops in the eighteenth century gathered, some on horses and some on foot, and marched through the streets. That's how this place got its name. Here too, in Parade, Jamaicans who resisted the colonial government were hanged and flogged. I remember resisting Mama. I remember my own flogging.

That night as I slept Mama whipped me. She had never whipped me so hard. She had never bruised my skin when she whipped me. I don't know what she whipped me with. I could not see it. It felt like a piece of plastic cord or a strong vine from a tree. I still don't know the real reason why. *Why Mama?*

I know Mama wanted me to stop seeing Robert. She couldn't stop me. She was angry, so, so angry the evening before the night, when I took a long time to return from the store. I don't know if that was the reason. Maybe it was everything. Maybe it was just me, Mama didn't know me any more, Mama couldn't love what I'd become. I prayed before falling asleep because something did not feel right that evening. My instinct was right. It was unexpected. Sudden. I felt as though my heart had stopped for a while or I was suffocating because I gasped for breath after the first strike.

My screams drummed, echoed, and filled the silence of the night. I don't like to remember that night.

A sting to my back startled me and another sting brought disorientation, and another sting woke me and another sting made me flinch and another sting opened my mouth and another sting pushed a scream and another sting dragged me from my bed and another sting brought me to my feet where I stood on the floor and tried, frantically, to block the whip with my hands in the dark. Darkness blinded my eyes. Mama blocked me. I couldn't run.

The rush of the whip swished as it whacked my flesh. Mama grunted between her strikes. "Bad child.

111

Rude child. I need to set you straight." The sting dug into my veins as the whip lifted into the air, it zinged past my ear and dug into my back again. I squealed a squeal to protest my pain, pain that surged through my back and into my veins.

Mama stopped flogging. I crawled back on my bed. Lying on my stomach, I stroked my tender back. Tracks of welts spread all over. My tender skin hurt against the mattress. I lay awake forever and then I somehow slept and awoke when daylight sneaked into cracks in the ceiling and gaped at me from the glass window. I made my bed and made my plans to escape. For the first time, I stole money from Mama. Her twenty dollars that I bought lunch with for Raquel and me.

At the park where I sit, a woman walks up to the bench and sits beside me. She peels an orange. Seeing the woman eating her orange reminds me that I'm hungry.

A man with a big red, yellow and green umbrella over a wooden cart sells what Jamaicans call sky juice. It is made of frozen syrup mixed with water in a clear plastic bag. He wears a hat on his head. The colors on the hat are the same as on the umbrella. The Rastafarian colors. Rastafarians take the colors from the Garvey movement. Red for the blood that martyrs have shed in the history of the Rastafarians; yellow or gold for the wealth of the homeland, Ethiopia, the promised land; and green for the beauty and vegetation of Ethiopia; and black for the color of Africans.

I pass the man with the cart. He sings the words, "Sky juice and box juice. Daughter, buy a juice from me, uh."

Thirsty from walking in the sun, I turn around and buy a sky juice. I take the sky juice and bite on one corner, making a hole in the bag and the cool sweet syrup squirts into my mouth. I drift along Princess Street. Later, I buy a beef patty. The hot ground spicy beef inside burns my tongue. I open my mouth and let my tongue cool before I take another bite.

Like a nomad, I wander from street to street searching for a place to rest. Not knowing where I'm going, I continue to drift—then, my gosh—from nowhere, a thought stops me. Why didn't I think of this before? She's just around the corner.

~~◆~~

In the center of her shed that surrounds her and the tin measuring cups, tin kerosene lamps and spices she sells, Mrs. Chan sits, showing off her goods, all ready to serve her customers. Seeing me, I know was definitely the last thing on her mind. Yet, the emotion on her face is not, "What the hell are you doing here?" Her smile, so beautiful, so welcoming and so warm makes her eyes linger softly on me.

Mrs. Chan rises from her wooden stool, and without saying a word she bends over the measuring cups and spices and I drop my bags from my hand and bend towards her and our arms reach around each other. We hug and we let go.

Here I am, standing right before her, legs shaking, with only one thing on my mind. Get to the point. I know what she'll say. She's too nice to say something else. Without telling her anything, I ask, "Can I stay at your house?"

Without asking a single question, with an uncomfortable smile and with pity in her eyes, Mrs. Chan says exactly what I knew she would say.

"Yes."

And she adds, "But I'll be here for a while. You can go home and stay there until I come. Just knock on the door."

"Mr. Chan home?" I ask.

"Yes," she says.

Mrs. Chan, part Black and part Indian, looks down and her two long plaits fall from behind her ears and rest on her chest. Her hair, the way she combs it, reminds me of mine, but mine is not so straight and not so long. Mrs. Chan grabs the bottom of the blue apron she wears over her floral dress that looks like a housecoat. She pushes her small hand into the apron pocket. Coins jingle against each other. Her slender fingers scoop the coins.

"I'll give you some bus fare. You know which bus to take, right?" Mrs. Chan stretches her hand toward me. Some shiny ten and five cents lay on her soft palm.

"I have money. Thanks," I say. I have more than enough to take me to Trench Town. Thanks to Smoker.

"See you soon."

"Ok," I say, barely opening my mouth.

I squeeze along the passage, passing other women talking and laughing, some negotiating and selling plastic mixing bowls, cups and plates, brooms and rakes, oranges and tangerines. Men sell peanuts and roasted corn, belts and t-shirts, fake gold rings and neck chains.

I imagine Mrs. Chan, almost as tiny as I am but not as strong as me. Her skin spreads softly over her tiny bones. She walks briskly. Her seventy-something-year-old body bends as she collects measuring cups and lamps and piles them into a black plastic bag. She does not put too many in. She slings the bag over one shoulder and carries it to work the next morning.

As I ride the bus, I imagine people walking in the park in Trench Town and children playing. I imagine Bob Marley, when he lived close by, flashing his locks, rocking his body, singing "Trench Town Rock" and "One Love." What will my life become here?

~~ ◆ ~~

"You here again?" Mr. Chan's skin on his forehead rises and wrinkles. He's part Chinese and part African. "Come in. Come in," he says. He nods and smiles. He removes the iron lock from the iron bars that cage the house.

"I'm back. Mama let me come back." I see no need to tell Mrs. and Mr. Chan that I had returned to Kingston a while ago, see no need to stir up any memory talking about where I was and what happened. I see the need to shut my mouth, because it's not like Mr. Chan cares about what I've been doing. All I know is that the two of them like me and I'm sure they are glad to have me here, especially because Andrea's son, Owen lives here too. Owen runs to me and sits on my lap.

Arriving home, Mrs. Chan smiles with me. She sits beside me. I think, by the way she's looking at me, Mrs. Chan feels sorry for me. She asks what I wish to do here and although the school year began already,

115

and although I wish for many things, I tell her this one.

"I would like to go to school."

"That's it?" she says, as if surprised, as if it's a small wish.

"Yes," I say.

If Mrs. Chan could see inside my body, she would see how my heart celebrates because I will get to finish high school. I lived with Cole and neither he nor Sally ever asked me if I wanted to go to school.

The next day, I awake early, anxious to register for school. I walk in the blazing sun to Kelly's Technical High school about a quarter of a mile from Mr. and Mrs. Chan's house. It's the closest high school to where I live. At the school, girls dress neatly in navy blue tunics and boys wear khaki pants, white shirts and gold and black-striped ties. They walk about the schoolyard and in the corridor. In the office, the secretary asks me why I want to switch from a normal high school to a technical high school. I tell her that I moved from the country to Kingston.

"That's why?" She asks as if she knows or as if she detects something else. All I'm thinking is that she is thinking that I ran away. I hope I'm not giving her a signal. Was my answer too stupid?

"It doesn't make sense," she says. "No one leaves a regular high school to go to a technical school."

"This is the closest high school to my house."

"I can't take you. You know there's a fee, can you pay?"

"Please, can you take me? I will do my work."

"Sorry, if you can't pay the fee we can't take you."

Tears drop. I walk from the office.

I tell Mrs. Chan what happened.

"St. Anne's Secondary School is not far away," Mrs. Chan says. You will only have to take one bus to Parade and walk from there to school. Andrea and Steve used to go there. I'm sure they'll take you. You just need school clothes."

I do not have to pay any fees there. In Jamaica, according to some people, a secondary school is inferior to a high school, but I do not care. Any school is better than no school. Like Trench Town, St. Anne's Secondary school stands in another rundown area not far from Parade.

At St. Anne's, the secretary scares me. "Are you Catholic?"

I'm not a Catholic. Mama told me that I wasn't baptized.

"Yes," I lie. "But my mother lost my birth certificate when she was moving."

"You mean your baptism certificate?"

"Yes. Yes," I lie again. I don't want to lie, but I have to right now.

"Do you have a transcript?"

"Yes," I say and fumble in my handbag for my transcript. I look away as the secretary looks at the grades on my transcript.

At Happy Grove High school, just before I ran away, the teacher had kicked me out of his math class. I didn't complete my courses. My homeroom teacher commented that my performance had deteriorated. I don't know the meaning of deteriorate. But I know it's not good. I feel embarrassed showing the transcript to her.

"Dear Lord, please save me," I pray to myself silently.

The secretary walks away and talks to a man. I can't hear what she's saying, but I don't want to hear anything bad.

17
Worries in Trench Town

"You can start tomorrow," the secretary says. She tells me the rules about the dress code.

I smile and say, "Thank you very much."

Back home, Mrs. Chan sends me across the street to a dressmaker who takes my measurement and later makes my school clothes or uniform: a white blouse, a green skirt, and a yellow tie. Two days later, I begin school.

After school each day and after completing my homework, with no laundry to do because a helper washes my clothes, no Mama to annoy me, no Andrea to love, no Raquel to visit, no Shernette to fight with, no Sally to scare me, less time watching television and not much to do in the house, boredom creeps up on me. To rid my boredom, sometimes I go to the cemetery across the street with Lee, a friend who lives near to me. We pick these little plums from trees that grow among the tombs. It's my first time eating these plums. The people here call them Chinese plums. They are small, round and green but when they are ripe, they are yellow. They are delicious.

The people here say at nights gunmen hide among the tombs and the trees. I'm not scared here even though people talk bad about Trench Town. People kill people who they really want to kill. I like the people here and they like me. Nobody bothers *me*.

I also play with Owen and write poems, short stories and songs. Also, my way-over-due period creeps into my bored mind. I want Robert to know what's going on. I won't mention anything about Cole. I write a letter.

Two weeks later, after coming home from school one afternoon, I find a letter on the table. Robert's name stands at the top with his Hector's River address and my name sits at the bottom with my Trench Town address. My heart thumps with excitement as I remove the letter from the table, plop on the sofa and grab a pencil from my school bag. I slide the pencil under one end of the flap that seals the letter. I imagine Robert writing the letter and walking to the post office to mail it. I gently roll the pencil under the seal not wanting to damage the envelope. On lined, white writing paper, Robert has replied to me.

He's coming to see me. I can move back to Hector's River to live with his family. Does he want to ruin my life? What will Mr. and Mrs. Chan think of me if they see him here? They will certainly get rid of me. I grab a notebook from my bag, rip a blank page from it and write back to Robert. I ask him not to come.

I stash Robert's letter in my brown bag, take one of Mrs. Chan's small white envelopes from a bundle she keeps on her dresser, fold the letter and shove it inside. I glide the glued flap of the envelope against my tongue, seal the letter, dash to the post office and mail it. *Please Lord, get this letter to Robert soon.* On my way back, I stop at the cemetery and hop from grave to grave. I'm hoping that if I'm pregnant, the baby will fall out somewhere between one of the graves and I can hide it among the Chinese plum trees. I hop and hop. I hop over big graves. I hop over small graves. I must stop hopping. The baby will not drop.

~~ ◆ ~~

On the veranda, staring through the burglar bars—oh no—Robert. Just a few days after I mailed the letter, Robert shows up—with two of his friends from Hector's River. The same Robert. Seeing him, my heart jumps as if it about to come out my mouth. My body shakes one big shake from a cold chill that surges in and out like electricity. Everybody will now know that I have or had a boyfriend. I'd imagined that when I see Robert again I would have run to meet him, run to give him a kiss when no one is looking, run to meet him because I would have been happy to see him. Now Robert has ruined my dream. Always. Robert, is always doing what he wants, never asking what I think.

He squints one eye and twists his lips to one side—I don't know how he does that—it's his charm smile, the one he had used many times to win me over to him. I remain seated inside, giving Robert a look of disapproval. My eyebrows curl, my eyes stare, speaking harsh unspoken words. He's there still standing, his hand resting on the top of the gate. He shrugs his shoulders as if he wants to say, "What's up? Aren't you coming to the gate?" I was so much in love with him, until now. Should I ignore him or invite him? Steve is not here, but what do I tell Mr. Chan who works at the back? I call Robert in with my fingers. He fumbles with the lock and the clanging of the iron echoes and Robert bobs toward me, all this time, staring at me. His two friends stay outside.

I open the burglar-barred door. I stare.

"We must be careful Robert. It's not my place. Sit." I direct Robert to sit in the chair beside mine.

"I miss you so much, Peaches."

"I miss you too."

"Please come back with me."

"I can't, Robert." I feel Mama whipping me in the night. I see my face with terror. I hear my screams. "I'm in school. I'm OK. I can't come back." My voice cracks.

What will my former teachers think about me? How will I face my former classmates and the other students in Happy Grove High School? "I can't come back."

"Yes, you can."

"No Robert, people must be talking about me."

"Not really. By the way, what if you are?"

"I don't know. I went to the doctor yesterday."

At Kingston Public Hospital, in a big room, on a long bench, I waited and waited for the free medical service, for the doctor to see me. Some people fanned themselves with thin books and papers from notebooks made into fans. Women sat with babies on their laps, some with babies to their breasts and some with babies hugging their necks. Hospital workers, one by one, called patients in. When my turn came, I walked in a little room. The doctor, overly gentle, examined my breasts. He softly asked how old I was, if they hurt, if they suffered injury and how long they were that way. I did not tell him I did not get my period for over five months, or that I could be pregnant. I did not want him to think I was a bad girl. He did not ask where my parents were. He gave me medication—some pills and said, "Take one three times a day for three days. That should get the swelling down and stop the pain."

"What did the doctor say?" Robert said anxiously.

"He just gave me some pills to take."

"For what?"

"My breasts."

"You didn't tell about that thing you miss."

"No."

"Why?"

"It's not your body, Robert."

"I know, but what if you *are*?"

"I don't know. I'm not sick. God will find a way to help me."

"Peaches, come back with me."

"No Robert. I'm not. I'm not. I'm not. Please go."

"I want to spend more time with you," says Robert. His eyes, with sadness, make me feel sorry for him. But I know I must stay strong. I have too much to lose.

"I can't. Do you want the people to throw me out of this house?"

"Don't you love me?"

"Of course I do."

"Can I kiss you?"

"No, we're in public."

"Robert, if you love me, please go. I don't want Mr. Chan to know you're here."

"OK. I'll go. Remember that I love you."

"I will," Robert says and stands. "But, can I spend more time with you?"

"No," I say. I must stay strong. I walk with Robert to the gate and as I'm about to let him out, Steve appears.

"Steve, this is my friend Robert," I say. "He's from Hector's River. Just came to look for me."

"That's cool," Steve says.

"Take care of her for me," Robert says.

"She's alright. Don't worry." Steve says.

"Write to me again," Robert says and turns away. He shrinks in the distance as I stare at him walking further and further away. I can't ruin my life for Robert a second time.

~~◆~~

Following my homework, which does not take a long time, I write more and more after school. I write more poems and more songs. No more letters to Robert. Steve sees me writing and asks what I write every day. I tell him I write mostly songs and poems. He asks to see one of my songs and I show him my favorite "Baby, I Love You." After reading my song, Steve says, "Good. Good song," and that if I really want to sing, he can ask his friend who's a singer, and who lives behind us, across from the park, to help me out.

The next day, Steve introduces me to Barry, a Rastafarian, a singer and guitarist in a reggae band who has traveled with his band to many countries in Europe. Steve says he was leaving and I thank him for introducing me to Barry. Steve is kind, despite beating up Andrea. Then, what I fear most, Barry asks me to sing here in the little park behind the Chan's house.

"I can't."

"How can you want to sing but you don't want to sing to me?"

"You're going to laugh."

"No. I don't do those kind of things. Just sing from your heart."

"OK, OK," I say and sing my song. My voice resonates not even like a poet but like a runaway string of words with no direction, climbing hills, running through valleys, getting stopped and being let go again.

You can't afford to do that baby / leaving me alone/ I have no one no love at all/ to make my dreams come true/ baby—

Barry interrupts, "Hey, hey. Hold it. Take your time. Don't eat up the words like that."

I want to disappear. "See, I told you."

"You just need some practice. Sing it like this," he sings the words.

I sing.
You can't afford to do that baby
Leaving me alone

He corrects me again.

Slowly, softly, serenely, Barry tames my voice and my song. The same words I just uttered now sound like different words. Strumming his guitar, timing every beat, singing every word, my song sounds like a real, real song. And Barry asks me to sing like he did and I'm now even more conscious of my voice. Sounding each sound, Barry asks me to repeat after him. In two hours, with the strumming on Barry's guitar, I can sing my song, not like a professional, but good enough. Barry tells me to meet him at the same place tomorrow.

~~ ♦ ~~

Back home, Steve sits in the living room, his eyes set on the television as I walk into the house.

"How was it?" he asks.

"It was good."

"That's good."

"Yeah, it was good."

"I read your letter."

"What letter?"

"The letter Robert wrote to you. Are you pregnant?"

The muscles in my face stiffen, I close my eyes briefly, I don't know what to say, how to respond and how to get out of this. Sneaky. Snake. Searching my stuff!

I stand still because I don't know if I should move. I wonder if Steve had mentioned anything to Mrs. Chan.

"Well." I sit in the sofa, a hand-length from him. "I don't know if I am."

"What if you are?"

"I don't think about it," I stare at the television. I will not let Steve know I'm upset with him for what he did. I will still talk to him, still laugh with him, still pretend I'm still the same girl he knows. I don't want to know if I'm pregnant because I'm scared of what will happen to me. If I am, I guess, one day, my belly will just pop right out and I will have to deal with it then.

Mrs. Chan walks into the living room. I sit, my back upright, my legs crossed at the ankles. Steve lies back on the sofa with a cushion under his head and hisses. I shiver. Mrs. Chan stands close to me, minding her own business, busy as always, pushing her hand, searching for what, I don't know, in a plastic bag. I don't mind the annoying rustling of the black plastic grocery bags many Jamaicans call scandal bags because once you touch one, everyone hears.

I do mind Steve's hiss as though he wants to pull one of us through a space between his teeth.

I don't know why he had to search my bag and talk about my problem as if he can fix it. It's none of his business. Steve hisses a longer hiss. Hearing the hiss, Mrs. Chan turns her head and her eyes fall on Steve.

"What's wrong?" she asks in a tone as if she talks to a baby.

Mrs. Chan might even tell me it's OK if I am. I'm sure she told that to Andrea when she got pregnant with Owen.

"Nothing, Granny," he says, and hisses softer than the other times.

I just shut my mouth.

"I'm going to sleep." Mrs. Chan eyes Steve from the corner of one eye, not in a pleasant way. My mind tells me to leave the room and walk behind her but I'm thinking Steve might be thinking I'm running away from answering his question. I'll leave, but in a minute or two.

I pretend I'm not paying attention to Steve, pretend that his shuffling on the couch does not bother me. "Peaches," he mutters, "Granny gone to—?" He shuffles on the sofa.

"I think so." Mrs. Chan is going to sleep. My body tenses. I'm thinking about what's next.

"Can we ...?"

He does not need to say another word for I know exactly where this conversation is going. I know what he seems to be hungering for. *How do I get out of this one, God?* Calmly, I pretend as if what he says does not bother my mind. I pretend that, it's not a big deal. In my heart and in my mind, I search for something believable to say.

Steve sits and stares at me. "What did you say?"

My stomach burns. I can't say no. Steve might do to me what Cole did. Find an excuse.

"Tomorrow night." The words spill from my throat. "I'm tired." I really want to tell Steve I'm not a plate of food ready for his meal.

"That's cool," Steve says, but I don't believe him. He's just staring at me with those eyes as if I'm supposed to feel sorry for him. Men are hungry sharks.

"I'm going to bed." I hurry to the bedroom.

~~◆~~

Lying on the bed across from the Chans' room, I worry about what Steve might do to me because I remember the time when I slept at my friend's house. It was a bad night. It was a long night.

Just before I turned fourteen, Amanda, my rich classmate, who lived in a big house, invited me for a sleepover. I told Mama that Amanda invited me to sleep over. Mama said no the evening after school when I asked her if I could go. But I begged and told her that Amanda is a good girl. "Please. Please Mama," I said, knowing that if I pestered her long enough she would say yes. She did say, "Yes. Yes! I don't like those sleep over business, but only for tomorrow." I felt happy because I had never before slept over at another friend's house.

After school the next day, I hopped on the bus with Amanda. Before going to sleep, Amanda told me I have to sleep in my own room. I thought Amanda would let me sleep on the same bed with her, but I didn't complain.

Urrrn, the door lock moaned from a turn. Clink. Clink. The hinges on the door creaked. I turned my head and opened my eyes. I clutched the sheet, yanked it over my head, and gawked through a little open space. A shadowy heavy person sat beside me on the edge of the bed. He touched my shoulders. "No. Please. Leave me alone." I cry. The shadow strolled out the door.

Clink, clink. The door opened again. More scared, I opened my eyes in the dark. A smaller head popped in the open door. It's not the same man. He lay beside me and talked to me and I didn't know what to do. I gripped the sheet to keep me covered and turned my back to the man. He asked what was wrong and I told him, "It's not right." He walked from the room. I was afraid that if I fell asleep something bad would happen to me. And the night, the awful night, seemed as if it would not end. By the time the third one walked in, I was tired from a lack of sleep, so I just cried in the night and I prayed in my mind for God to save me to let nothing bad happen to me. In my mind, I cried for Mama to come and rescue me, and for the man to go away, and for the new day to release the night. After a while, the man strolled from the room.

Here, I don't know what to do with Steve. What will I do tomorrow night? I can't complain to the Chans about their grandson.

~~ ♦ ~~

Two-hour singing lessons with Barry, free of course, now consume my boredom. I look forward to leaving school each day, doing my homework, and then meeting Barry in the park. Sometimes I take Owen with me. Barry says when my singing gets much better than it is, he will introduce me to the band.

The same things happen every day. I sing and Barry corrects me and strums on his guitar and then we say our goodbyes. Then I go home and Steve asks me again, and I say "Tomorrow night," again and rush to bed right after Mrs. Chan does.

The big day arrives. Barry takes me to a room filled with musical instruments: drums and cymbals, guitars and amplifiers. Rastafarians welcome me with handshakes, hugs and smiles. I bring my friend, Lee, the girl I pick plums in the cemetery with and another little girl.

I stand on a stage before a mike. Guitars strum, cymbals clang, trumpets blow, drums pound, and bodies rock as I sing.

> *You can't afford to do that baby, leaving me*
> *alone*

I have no one, no love at all to make my dreams come true
Baby you may not seem to know how much I love you so
Baby you may not seem to know how much you've hurt me so
Oh, oooohh baby, you know I love you, oh yeah

Baby, baby, baby, you know I love you from the start
Baby, baby, baby, please don't you ever break my heart
I need you now, I need you now, I need you right by my side
I need you now, I need you now, I need you all through the night
Oh, baby, you know I love you, oh yeah. –
There's not a day and not a night that everything I do seem to be right
'Cause baby without you in my arms everything seems to be way out of sight
I know that one day baby, you'll come running back to me
I know on that day baby, I won't accept your apology
'Cause baby, you know I love you, but you went away

Baby, baby, baby, you know I love you from the start
Baby, baby, baby, please don't you ever break my heart

I need you now, I need you now, I need you
right by my side
I need you now, I need you now, I need you
all through the night
Oh, baby, you know I love you, oh yeah. –

The next evening, a group of young children join me in the park as I sing and Barry plays the guitar. The following evening, the choir of children sings the chorus of my song outside my gate as I get ready to meet Barry. I can't believe it. The children sing my song as if they'd heard it on the radio. My head swells with joy and pride and I smile with the children. I now know I'll definitely be a singer. The next day, I write a letter to Tuff Gong, Bob Marley's record studio. The next week, I receive a reply with a date for an audition. The next day, after the letter from Tuff Gong, I share my news with Barry. The next Saturday, Barry and I meet in the park. As usual, I sit next to him.

I feel a little uneasy as Barry looks intently at my face, as if it is the first time he's seen it. And the fact that Barry doesn't sing or play the guitar he cradles and the fact that he doesn't ask me to sing, worries me. I don't know how to break this tension. Barry places his guitar on the grass. "Sit." Barry pats one leg, indicating that I sit on his lap.

"Noooo." I say. But I really want to say, "Are-you-crazy-in-the-head?"

Pigeons flutter over us in the cool of the day.

I have never seen Barry like this. I feel queasy, and then I don't know why, but my instinct says *run home*. Confused, I run from the park and through the narrow passage. I run through the gate.

~~◆~~

Days come and go when I longed to see Barry, to hear him play, to help me train my voice, to help me become the singer I wanted to become. But I know, with all my heart and all my desires that I made the right decision. I saw Barry yesterday. The most polite thing we did was to give each other a smile. Nothing else. I have to stop turning men into sharks. I need to change. I don't know how.

Nightmares haunt me: Amanda's house, the man who walked through the window, Cole and Frank. I dream about Steve and what he might do.

Steve's getting impatient, telling me that I keep telling him the same story every night. The same story is, "Tomorrow night." But what else can I tell him? I'm afraid to tell him no. I'm tired of Steve nagging me every night and I'm tired of rushing off to bed behind Mrs. Chan every night just to avoid fulfilling my promise.

I have tried to keep away from Mama's relatives living here in Kingston. I purposely do so because I don't want my business going back to Hector's River. But as the pressure to yield to Steve goes on and on, I know I have to leave this place. Soon.

By mid-morning, without telling my classmate, Sandra, my business, I hurry from school. I find a public telephone to call my cousin, Vanessa, who works at a bank uptown. I ask Vanessa to ask Mrs. Bartley, a woman who had paid me to braid her hair, if I could live with her. My cousin tells me to hold on and after a few minutes, she returns and tells me that

Mrs. Bartley said I should call back tomorrow because she has to discuss the issue with her husband.

~~♦~~

Getting the courage to tell Mrs. Chan I'm leaving is very painful. After all, she has been so kind, loving, and respectful to me and has treated me so well and now I will appear ungrateful for all she's given me. I mull over how I will break the news to Mrs. Chan. I wouldn't have the nerve to look at Steve any more and Steve would probably despise me. Many alibis swim in my head but only one seems to be good because it's not a lie and I don't think it will hurt her feelings.

My legs jerk as I allow Mrs. Chan to eat her dinner, put away the bags she brought home from work, take her shower, and sit down. And for some good reason, at least for me, Steve is not home and Mr. Chan stays at the back of the house. One, two, three, do it now, I say to myself. I open my mouth but the words cannot come out. Again. One, two, three.

"Mrs. Chaaan," my voice trails, low and nervous.

"Uhn."

"I want to tell you something."

"Uhn." Mrs. Chan sits upright.

"I'm leaving."

Mrs. Chan's eyes widen. I had anticipated this moment. Feeling sad for Mrs. Chan is exactly what I wanted to avoid. It would have been better if I had just written a note and fled. She will never understand how sad I feel to leave too.

"Why?" she says.

And this is where my alibi comes in. I had anticipated *Why?* so I reply, "This... is... a bad area... to live. "

"Oooooh," she gasps. Mrs. Chan closes her eyes, lowers her head and gasps, "Oooooh," again.

So be it for my brilliant alibi. I had not anticipated this feeling, not this pain on her face. *Yes, my great honest alibi.* Now it's clear to me that it's wrong to tell her that the place she knows, the place she has lived almost all her life, the place she has sheltered me in, is bad.

"Anything bad happened to you here?"

"Noooo."

"People don't just go around killing people, you know."

"I know."

"No one died here since you're here."

"I know."

"So why?"

I say nothing.

"I can't stop you," she says. "But I want you to know this. Are you listening?"

"Yes."

"It's not *where* you live," she says. "It's *how* you live. Doctors come out of this place. Nurses come out of this place. Teachers come out of this place. Bob Marley, even though I don't care about reggae, came out of this place. So it's not where you live, I'll tell you that, but it's how you live."

I can't say anything else as Mrs. Chan's bright eyes fade. She folds her lips into silence. Her face shows sadness. I know she knows that I have already made up my mind or else I wouldn't mention leaving her home.

I have no right to destroy her relationship with her grandchild. I will let her hold on to what she knows or thinks of him. After all, maybe I'm wrong, but there's no crime in trying to get something you want. Steve did not force me to do anything. All I had to say was no, but I didn't.

"I thank you for all that you've done," I say, "I really appreciate your kindness. I'll leave after school tomorrow."

"I won't be here. But take care of yourself."

"I'll tell Mr. Chan that I'm leaving."

Mrs. Chan nods her head. I know she'll never forgive me for being so ungrateful. Some people say when you do bad things to others that bad things will come back to you. I hope God will forgive me because I don't need any more bad things to happen to me as I move to another home.

18
Lacy Panties and Brassieres

Holding my bags, I step from the bus and barge into the bank, glancing all around to see the kind woman who will take me in her home. A clock ticks and tocks, coins clink and clank, machines ding and dong and slippers flip and flop. Customers scurry in and out the door, tellers greet them with smiles and the air-conditioned room cools heated bodies. I glance at my uniform, my brown shoes and white socks, making sure I look clean. Look good. Pretending to be bold, I purse my lips, stroll to the counter, smile back at the teller and tell her I am here to see Mrs. Bartley.

A poised hip-swinging, shoulder-swaying Mrs. Bartley ambles towards me. With her head lowered, she casts a look on me with smiling eyes. My chest and face tighten. I am trying, desperately, to relax my strained smile.

"I'll be finished in one hour, so you can sit and wait over there," Mrs. Bartley says as I do nothing else but stare and smile and hope and hope she does

137

not ask me if I ran away or why am I not with my mother.

I must seem clownish with this everlasting smile. I feel clumsy and it's not because I'm thinking that I'm about to bang Mrs. Bartley's forehead with mine as I nod, but because I feel as though I'm losing my grip on the two plastic bags in my hand. It's my nerves. Just my imagination because as I tighten my grip more, I notice the bags were not even near slipping from my grip and maybe my head wasn't even so close to Mrs. Bartley. I must seem really stupid.

I wait as tellers count, customers chat and money flutters. My knees, these uncontrollable knees, knock side to side. I talk to myself, telling myself to be good and to behave myself so that this family will keep me.

Time passes fast in this busy bank. Mrs. Bartley, clutching a small handbag under one arm, ambles out to meet me. As I see her, the same strained smile—I can't help it—appears on my face again. She holds my hands, and the feeling, the touch of her hands on mine—sweet, warm and tender—helps me to relax. I can't believe it—just the way she touches me, I can feel it, and I can tell that she has much love in her heart. She has a big heart.

"It's nice to see you," Mrs. Bartley says. "It's been a while."

"Yeah, it's been a while," I repeat.

"Joseph will soon be here."

"OK," I say.

"Let's go outside."

"OK," I say.

She does not pry. She's not nosy. I'm so glad she's not asking questions about my life.

As soon as we step outside, Mrs. Bartley's husband, Joseph, drives and stops before us. Three girls and one boy sit in the car. Two of the girls, Marla and Laura, and the little boy, Larry, are the Bartley's children, and Nadia, is her niece. I had met them before when I braided Mrs. Bartley's hair. I like Laura, the younger daughter, and Larry and Nadia too. Marla, maybe because she's older, maybe because I can't pretend to like someone if I don't, probably detected I was not as fond of her as I was of the other children. I just don't know exactly why I didn't like her as much as I liked the other kids.

The children look at me. Laura, Larry and Nadia, all smile. Marla is kind of serious.

"Move over," Mrs. Bartley tells the children. "Let Peaches sit at the end." When I drove with them before, the rule was that the bigger children sit at the windows at the back or in the front seat when one adult is absent. The children squeeze together as they make room for me. I squeeze my body, bringing my arms almost together and resting my hands in my lap. I stare out the window. As the car exits from Trafalgar Boulevard and turns, close to the Bartley's house, I gaze.

Big, mostly white houses, line the streets. Neatly trimmed green, green grass and an array of beautiful flowers decorate the front yards. Cars, big and little cars, sit on driveways. Excitedly, the girls, even Marla, point to the houses.

"That's where Natasha Manley lives, the former prime minister's daughter," says Marla.

"That's where Leoni Forbes lives." They point to the home of the famous Jamaican actress. They continue to point out houses and names of people and I begin to think how fortunate I am that I will be living among Jamaican aristocrats.

~~ ◆ ~~

Mrs. Bartley prepares dinner in the kitchen. I observe. I even try helping out, asking where I get the seasoning: fresh thyme, seasoning salt, black pepper, garlic and onions. I wash the rice, watch it boil, turn down the heat and let it simmer. Mrs. Bartley stews beef. She adds carrots, red and green sweet peppers, garlic and onions. It's as if we are all working on one big project, everybody doing a part—well, except Mr. Bartley, who relaxes in a chair in the living room, his eyes focused on the *Jamaican Gleaner*, nothing disturbs him. The girls—all of them—set the table, knives and forks and plates in their appropriate places. Living with Mama, we didn't really set the table before eating. There was no need for that. We shared the food in our plates and grabbed our forks or whatever utensil we needed.

With the food on the table, Laura calls, "Daddy, dinner."

In Hector's River, I notice that the well-to-do people's children and some of my friends call their parents Mommy or Mummy and Daddy. The poor people's children called their parents Mama and Papa. In this house, the children call their parents Mommy and Daddy. I will call them Mr. and Mrs. Bartley.

Buffet style. I think all these utensils, bowls and extra things for this and that just create more work. Somebody will have to wash the dishes. I hope I don't have to do this every day.

Steam rises from the bowl of rice, the bowl of beef and the bowl of green beans in a row in the middle of the wooden dining room table. Laura stretches for the rice before her. Mr. Bartley reaches for the beef next to him. Marla asks Mr. Bartley to pass the beef to her after he scoops out his share and Mrs. Bartley and I just wait until everyone takes their share of the food.

The taste of garlic dominates all the seasoning in this stew and although I do not like the smell or the taste of garlic, this stew tastes delicious. Sweet. With my mouth closed, I'm trying to show that I know how to eat around the table, I savor the taste of the food.

"This is good." Mr. Bartley nods his head. "Did you cook it, Peaches?"

"Oh, no," I say and chuckle.

"Well, I'll take credit for what I did," Mrs. Bartley says in sing-song voice.

"Oh Mom, your food is always good," Marla says in a kind of 'good' English voice.

Except for Mr. and Mrs. Bartley, who throw in a little Jamaican language every now and then, and Nadia, who once lived in the countryside like me, the Bartley's children, apart from their accent, all talk as if the Jamaican language is foreign to them. They don't speak it. They speak "proper" English. Even most poor people in Jamaica do not want their children to speak Jamaican. I'll have to tone-down—or is it tone-up?—my language. I'll try not to say much. I don't want to give anyone the opportunity to ask me questions that I would not want to answer.

I don't bring up anything about my used-to-be family in Hector's River. I don't even talk about

Andrea whom I love so much. To even say or admit that I had a boyfriend would be like chopping off my head, especially in this family where they all seem as though they've never committed a sin in their entire lives.

After dinner, I wash the dishes, braid the three girls' hair and complete my school work. Nadia has the healthiest hair, but the biggest head and the thickest hair, and I hate combing it. I don't tell her because I like her, plus it's my duty to comb it anyway.

"You've got a lot of hair." That's all I say.

"I've got the most hair," she replies, as if I should be happy for her hair.

At night, it's obvious love runs deep in this family. Mr. and Mrs. Bartley kiss each other. The children hug and tell each other goodnight and I start to do as they do. Mama always said, "When you're in Rome, you do as the Romans do." I'll get used to all of this. Plus, it's not bad to copy good things. As the oldest of the girls, I sleep on top of a triple bunk bed, Nadia beneath me and Laura beneath Nadia. Marla sleeps on a single bed across the room.

Mornings, I awake at 6:00 a.m., before everyone. I make breakfast for everyone. I have to get to school before 8:00 a.m. I don't go to the same school as the Bartley's children.

I return home before everyone by 2:00 p.m. I cook dinner when I get home as I'm the first one home. In Hector's River, whoever has more time, does whatever work there is to do. I'll do the same here.

Work is plentiful here with so many children. I pick up Larry sometimes on my way from school, cook dinner while I do my homework and when everyone gets home we eat dinner and I comb the girls' hair before I go to sleep.

On weekends, Saturday mornings, the family wakes up early. Then the girls and I wipe, dust, and polish the dining table, chairs, the floor and the handrails on the sofa. Laura does most of the dusting. Marla polishes the furniture. I polish the floor while Nadia shines it. She does not fall on her knees as I did in Hector's River. She uses the electric shiner. This is first one I've ever seen.

But this place, apart from all the work we must do, is paradise. No one shouts. The children don't get beatings. Yet they are well behaved. They obey their parents. On weekends, the Bartleys always take us somewhere. Sometimes we go to movies, or orchid shows, which Mrs. Bartley does as a hobby, and I watch her with all her uppity friends talk about flowers. To me, the orchids are just orchids. I don't see the big deal why these women gasp when they see different ones.

Sometimes, when Mr. and Mrs. Bartley are not home, I teach the children songs they don't know. They love the songs I teach, especially this one: "Mama Look A Boo Boo." The children laugh and laugh, and ask me to sing again and again until they learn it.

They sing the song and make faces at each other.

We also sing: "Day O."

When I sing this song, a part of me wants to go home, back to Hector's River. But I don't tell the children. I just want them to have fun.

One day, when Mrs. Bartley returns home, she calls us. I worry. Mrs. Bartley has a serious look on her face.

"The neighbors heard you singing," she says.

I'm thinking I'm in big trouble, teaching the kids bad songs and disturbing the neighbors.

We stand still and listen.

"Mrs. Scott and her husband like your singing." Mrs. Bartley smiles. "Mrs. Scott thinks you should get some singing lessons and sing professionally."

"Wow!" I gasp.

"Maybe I should sing more," Laura says.

I'm so relieved.

On Sundays, always, we go to church. Mrs. Bartley loves God. The children do too. I'm glad I can go to church again. After church, we go home, change our clothes and eat roast beef, barbeque chicken, spareribs or whatever I prepare with Mrs. Bartley. After an early dinner, we go to the beach or fishing or visit the Bartley's relatives in the city or drive for miles to the countryside to visit their other relatives. There's always something to entertain us. I guess this is what good families do. I don't know, but I suppose.

And ironically, in Hector's River, I washed my clothes, but sometimes Mama or Shernette did the washing. And Mama washed and iron other people's clothes, but here, a lady does what Mama does. The lady washes and irons my clothes. If Mama knew, I think she would say I'm "living the good life."

~~ ◆ ~~

One day at school I feel sick and my belly hurts and I feel sicker and my belly hurts more and I want to go home and I hurry home after school and I lie in bed as cramps wrench my belly. I cry and squirm. And then something warm and wet runs between my legs. I rush to the washroom. My monthly friend, who had disappeared, who had made me worried and who I decided to forget ever was a part of my life, is here, bright red and warm and plenty. Just like that.

"Thank you, God. Thank you," I say. "I'm not pregnant. Thank you. You answered my prayers."

I'm wondering if my period didn't return because of the beating. The shock. I know I've heard people in Hector's River say that if something bad happens to someone that it can mess up their minds. Maybe the beating messed up my mind. Some people say when something shocks your mind it can cause trauma. Oh, well. I'm just happy now because I don't know what I would do with a baby. I guess I would become a teenage mother as Andrea and Mama were.

Although I worried for months, I had gotten used to not seeing my friend, not having to deal with her, not having to worry about getting something to wear. But I can't complain, in this house, I can take care of her. She comes at a good time. I wash and grab a pad from Mrs. Bartley's collection. I now wear real sanitary napkins and I don't have to worry about how I can get or pay for them. In a way, I'm glad it didn't come when I lived with the Chans because I would have to ask them for money to buy pads. Mrs. Bartley won't mind me using her pads. I know. I'm part of the family. She's a nice lady.

~~♦~~

I don't ask Mrs. Bartley for everything I need. The shoes I wear to school are old. I ask John for money to buy a new pair of shoes. I tell Mrs. Bartley that John gave me the shoes. When John and I lived in Hector's River, I could have never imagined that John would one day buy me a pair shoes.

Mama could barely afford to buy us shoes, especially shoes for school. I walked barefooted to school a number of times. But, walking barefooted to school was not as embarrassing as the day John wore the pair of flip-flops he made for himself.

John got a piece of rope and cut rubber, the shape of his feet, from an old car tire. He made three holes into the carved-out footprints, cut the ropes, pushed them through the holes, tied knots at the bottom and walked into his new flip-flops.

One evening, as I walked by my friend Raquel's house with John, Raquel's sister, Pam, stood near the gate at the laneway. She pointed and laughed. I didn't know what the big deal was. But she pointed at John's feet, his flip-flops. I felt sad for John and I felt like crying. But I laughed, hiding my shame and John's pain and shame. I said, "John has a new invention." John didn't say a word. He looked at Raquel's laughing sister and he smiled. But the smile wasn't real.

When we arrived home, John kicked off his slippers into the mosquito fire. In no time, stench from the burning rubber filled the area around us as smoke rose while the tire and rope sizzled and smoldered in the fire. John walked barefooted until Mama bought him another pair of shoes.

Life can change. Yes. Now John can afford to buy shoes for me and for himself.

~~ ◆ ~~

My favorite time comes after school, on the days when I have the house to myself. I wish the house were mine. From Mr. Bartley's stack of records, two have become my favorites. I close the windows and the blinds, release my hair from elastic bands and plaits, let it flow over my back and my shoulders and blast the stereo, killing every other sound when I play and play "Chiquitita" by Abba. I close my eyes and hug myself as I dance and dance, feeling joints and muscles move in my body, then I put myself in a place I call my Heaven and I feel the drums, the guitars and all the other instruments beat inside me and waves of emotion wash over me and in one moment I'm laughing and laughing and the next I'm crying and crying as I take in the beats from the instruments. And "Fernando" plays. And I cry again, to Barbara Streisand, to "The Way We Were." This time I sit, close my eyes and listen to the soft sounds and the sad words. I don't know for sure if I'm cherishing my memories of Mama, Robert or my friends in Hector's River. Maybe I want to feel sad because I don't know why I do this to myself, but it feels good to feel sad. It does.

As months glide by, I'm beginning to get bored hearing "Chiquitita" and "The Way We Were." Now I play "Dancing Queen." I don't feel so sad any more, but I'm lonely. To battle my loneliness, I'm now writing a screenplay—one about a poor girl who falls in love with a rich guy. I'm also writing about men and women arguing over housework—not that I've seen this with my mother—because she's never lived with a man since she left my father. But I think this must be common. Although Mr. Bartley is very nice, he doesn't do any housework. Or he doesn't do it in my presence.

When I'm bored, I also search the Bartley's bookshelves. I want to know what Mr. Bartley finds so interesting in those books. He reads a lot. He talks about Boris Pasternsk's *Dr. Zhivago*. I scan some of the pages to see what's interesting, but I'm not interested in anything about Russia. I pick up Frantz Fanon's *Black Skin White Masks* because I don't understand what mask the writer talks about in the book. Gosh, this book is about Black and White people and it has too many big words for my little mind.

I experiment with Mr. Bartley's shaving powder too. I don't know how magical this Magic Shaving Powder that sits in the bathroom really is, but I have to try it too. After all, Mr. Bartley uses it to shave his face. I must try it. The best area is down here where there's enough hair. I remove my underwear. I won't spread it all over. I empty some of the Magic Shaving Power, mix it with water and spread it on one side. Wow! My hair is melting. Just like that. I guess it's really magic and I must wipe it off before it does more damage. Oh my goodness! I'm shinny bald on one side, but I'm not going to put this thing on the other side. Good for me, now, a day after, I itch as though stinging nettle invades my underwear.

I put on Mrs. Bartley's clothes, too, when I'm bored. Her fancy dresses, her lacy panties and brassieres and I pretend to be like her, rich in nice clothes with three of her own kids and two orphans—Nadia and me. I think I've tried on all the clothes in Mrs. Bartley's closet. So I look for more. What's up there, in the closet, on the shelf? Things nicely stashed away? I dig and dig, making sure I put back things in their right places.

There's a book.

A white book.

A big book.

A new book.

It's under some clothes and stuff.

Why do the Bartleys put a book in the closet? The others are on the bookshelves. I have to see this book. I dig and pull. Wow! New. It seems as though no one has ever touched this book.

Oh-my-goodness!

What's this? I've never seen such a book with such a title in all my life. This must be much better than my *Love Verses* book.

Oh goodness. What's in there? I stare at the clean cover. I have to read it and learn some more about it.

I grab the book and jump from the chair I stood on and together, the book and I land on the floor and I sit with my back against the Bartleys' bed and prop the book on my lap. I flick the front cover. My mouth opens. My eyes widen. I cover my mouth with one hand. My eyes cannot believe what I'm seeing. Ooooo! Ooohhhh! Whoever invented these whatever—? Gymnastics. Man and woman. Bending and twisting. Lying and standing. Oooooh! I can't wait until tomorrow. I must take this precious book to school to show my friends. I close the closet and walk from the room. I stash the book in my school bag.

19
Only for Married People

At break, in the classroom, my four close friends, Paul, Sandra, Amy and Jessica, surround me to view and experience the pleasure I discovered yesterday in the book. *The Joy of Sex.* I wait for the teacher and my other classmates to vanish from the classroom. I reach nervously into my bag for the book, pull it out and place it on the desk before me. I'm about to open the book and already four pairs of eyes, virgins to the contents, eagerly wait. I want to tease them more, so with a slow ease I lift the first page halfway and then stop.

"Come on," Sandra says.

I turn the page and "Oooooh," they gasp. Their surprise, shock and excitement fill the classroom.

I smile. "Wanna see more? That's nothing." I turn the page.

"Wicked," Paul says.

"Oh my goodness," Sandra says.

Each turning of the page shocks and excites them and "Ohhh" and "Ahhhhhhh" and "Wow" and

"Wicked" and "Oh my goodness" and "Lord have mercy" continue to the end of the book.

"Can I borrow it?" Paul begs.

"Promise to God." I lower my head and cast my eyes at Paul. "Promise me you won't show it to anyone else."

"Can I borrow it, too?" Sandra asks.

"Me, too," Amy and Jessica say together.

Because Paul asked first and Sandra second and Amy and Jessica together, I decide to loan the book to Paul first and Sandra second. Amy and Jessica fuss about who should be next to take the book. While they argue, Paul grabs the book, runs to his seat and shoves it into his school bag.

"Geez!" Amy looks at her watch. "We are going to miss break."

Out of fifteen minutes, we only have three left for break. We rush from the classroom.

Paul takes the book home and returns it as promised. The next day I pass it on to Sandra. Before the loan period ends, Paul giggles with me more. By the time I receive the book from Amy, who kept it over the weekend because she got it on Friday, Paul talks to me even more.

But I can't help thinking about the state of the book. My friends feasted well on it. The Bartleys will definitely know someone has been messing with their precious secret book. Some of the once crisp, clean, pages now show signs of mishandling and the cover is not as clean as it was.

I call my four friends and ask them why in Jesus' name they didn't take better care of the book since it did not belong to them or even me. And they all begin to blame one another, talking about who lent it

151

to whom and in what condition and who did what to it.

~~◆~~

I play "Chiquita," wipe the cover of the book and push it back to its hiding spot. My mind has captured all the poses so I don't need to see the book any more. I'm hoping the Bartleys will not look at the book again for a long time, maybe when I'm dead and lying in my grave—if I die before them—because they will know that I must be the culprit. If they discover their soiled book, they might also think it could be the washer-lady. I don't think they would confront the washer-lady or me. If they ask me about the book—if they will have the nerve to—because I don't know how they would ask me—I could deny it. Imagine them asking me, "Did you search my closet?" "Did you behold the sacred, only for married people, *Joy of Sex*? Do you know how disappointed we are that you would do this?" The Bartleys would not want me to imagine those acrobatic things they do in their bedroom. Maybe God will make them forget they had such a book.

~~◆~~

Paul starts asking me if I have a boyfriend.

"As a matter of fact," I joke with Paul in a polite voice, "I don't think it's any of your business."

"It's my business to know," says Paul, dark-skinned and handsome, "because I'm interested in you."

152

During breaks, when Sandra lines before the snack counter, Paul leaves the company of his male friends, walks over to where I stand and tries to talk "boyfriend-girlfriend" talk to me.

As well dressed as he usually is, and as neatly combed as his hair usually is, and as much as he flashes his dollar bills before me, I still don't care about Paul. He's a show-off, always walking like he's cool and acting as if he can get any girl he wants. But more than anything, *I don't want a boyfriend*. I don't want to mess up my life with the Bartleys.

I am getting more popular with my friends because I'm no longer living in Trench Town, or the ghetto as many call it. When I lived downtown, Jessica didn't talk much to me. Once she found out I lived uptown, in a good neighborhood, we grew closer or she liked me more. Also, I'm one of the brightest in the class and I do my work and my homeroom teacher likes me. Too, I'm cool for showing *The Joy of Sex* to my friends.

Paul bothers me every day. "Can I talk to you?" he asks.

This mid-morning break, rays from the sun heat the square, concrete-walled schoolyard. Sandra rushes to the bathroom. I stand silently near one corner of the schoolyard and sip chocolate milk. Paul ambles toward me. Gosh, not Paul again.

Outside the school tells a story of a place in need of the government's attention. It is adorned with rusty zinc and peeling concrete fences, and damaged roads and sidewalks. Old political strife—like Trench Town—intermingled with territorial boundaries awakens at nights. People die from bullets. Poverty bleeds through this area's veins.

And close to it, downtown Kingston, Parade, and other adjoining streets were better too. Under British colonial rule, there were bright colors, wealthy merchants, law and order, though cruel at times. Now it appears as though the good life from this area has gone. But I'm sure, people are still happy.

Paul walks the cool-boy skip-walk, one hand buried in his side pants pocket, the other swinging to and fro by his side, his body twists with each stride.

"Why don't you want to talk to me?" Paul says.

"No reason."

"You're too nice for me?"

"Never said that."

Paul pushes me against the concrete wall in the corner where two walls meet. I cower into the wall and stare into Paul's eyes. Paul restrains me with one hand pressed against my chest.

"Stop," I say.

"You think you're too nice for me?"

"No."

"I have something in my pocket."

Boys and girls play. Greens, whites, yellows and khakis move. They don't see us.

Paul reaches in his pocket.

"You want to see what I have in my pocket?"

I say nothing. Something vile, I know, is going on inside Paul.

Slowly, Paul pulls his hand from his pocket and I glance something silver and black. Paul flicks open a little penknife before my face. I stiffen.

"I can scar your pretty face," Paul says. "A nice, pretty, telephone cut." Paul sticks the tip of the knife at my right ear and draws it lightly along my cheeks to the corner of my mouth. Paul snaps the blade back into its place and shoves the penknife back into his pocket. He walks away.

There's a trend, especially here in the poor areas of Kingston, when there's conflict between people, one person may do something to hurt the other. Telephone cuts, meaning scars that run from the ears to the mouth as though holding a telephone are growing, though not at an alarming rate. Acid attacks are growing too. People want to leave bad memories, scars, disfigurement, and trauma. I don't want a scarred face. I've disobeyed my mother and traded my life in Hector's River for this one. I've made some stupid decisions. But I know when I should fight. I breathe hard and I drag myself to the girls' washroom. I wash my face.

The bell rings. In class, I look behind me and see Paul at his desk moving his pen across his paper, probably sketching something crazy. But I have things more worrisome on my mind.

20
Maybe I Should Tell Them

Christmas waits, but a few days away and the Bartleys talk about putting up and decorating the Christmas tree they store in the closet. I'm excited. Mama could never afford a Christmas tree. But I'm scared. Do they look at *The Joy of Sex* during the Christmas season when they take out the Christmas tree? Is it a once-a-year book? A Christmas treat? Dear God, I'm really, really in trouble. Great, getting myself in trouble is just great. Maybe I should tell them I could put up the tree after school. No. They might become suspicious.

"I can put up the Christmas tree after school on Monday." My words fly across the living room.

That's kind of you," Mrs. Bartley says. "Have you ever put up a Christmas tree?"

"No. But I think it should be easy. I'm good with my hands."

"It's OK, Peaches," Mr. Bartley says. His eyes move across the room and rest on me. "It's Saturday and since we're all here today, we can all work together. We'll put up the tree together. It's faster. It's more fun."

God, I need your mighty wings to protect me, I say to myself.

Walking backwards from the room, Mr. Bartley carts the box from the bedroom and places it in the middle of the living room. Maybe tonight, I worry. Maybe tonight he'll get the book.

All of us, including Mr. Bartley—he was right about working together—put up the Christmas tree. We don't work fast, but because we all helped out, the tree now stands on its own beside the television in the living room. A crystal angel shines on top of the tree, red lights twinkle all over, silver strips shimmer along the branches and red ornaments dangle between them.

Another Saturday has come. For the past week, I have worried about the book, but I haven't heard a single word about it from anyone. I hope the Bartleys don't use it at Christmas. I don't think I'm off the hook yet. I pray and I hope that the prayers I prayed last week worked.

~~ ◆ ~~

Mrs. Bartley and I, like a mother and daughter in the kitchen, make a small sample cake from the cake mixture. The heavy, fruit-laden Christmas cake tastes delicious. We can all try the sample cake before Christmas. Since it turned out great, we can now bake the real cakes.

In the kitchen, baking tins collect the cake mixture Mrs. Bartley and I pour into them. We place them in the oven. Minutes later, the baking cakes release the strong scent of their ingredients: alcohol—rum and wine; dried fruits—prunes, raisins, cherries, currants and lemon rind; and spices—cinnamon, nutmeg and vanilla all mixed with sugar, flour and butter. The scent drifts from the kitchen to the other rooms in the house, it escapes out the doors and windows and lingers in the house and teases our appetites.

In Hector's River, I remember, each Christmas Mama trekked to Aunt Patty's house to bake because we did not have an oven. Shernette, my cousin Jane and I went with Mama. We took turns helping to mix the sugar and the butter, the longest and hardest process. Once the sugar becomes liquid, everything else becomes easier. Maybe Mama has baked her cakes already, she has shared the sample with Bridgette and Shernette and maybe the other cakes are sitting on the dining table, and they are waiting for everyone to eat them on Christmas Day.

Christmas Day. Everyone here receives a gift or two. The children thank their parents. I thank the Bartleys too.

I think again about the years in Hector's River when all I wanted was a doll for Christmas, but Mama couldn't afford one. So I made my own dolls from big bottles and small bottles and different colored bottles. I uprooted grass, fine and long to make the doll's hair. I liked to comb the long grass hair. I parted it in sections, braided it and put rubber bands at the end of the plaits to keep the plaits together. Sometimes I made ribbons from scraps of cloth. I tied the ribbons into the grass hair.

I even made soft dolls from cloth, with scraps of material or bits of sponges. I made the eyes and eyebrows with black thread, the nose with brown thread and the lips with red thread. For the hair, I gathered my hair or Mama's hair or my sisters' hair from brushes and combs. I pasted on the hair with chewed chewing gum. I did not comb human hair as hard as I combed the grass hair because the human hair pulled out of the gum and came off the doll's head. I left the human hair in an Afro.

Then, one Christmas, after leaving my red bobby sock on the headboard of the bed, I pushed my head through the window, I looked at the sky, saw the stars and the moon. I saw a man sitting in the moon. The wind blew the thin white curtain over my face. I pushed the curtain aside. I said, "Man in the moon, make Santa Claus come to my room." I pulled my head inside, pulled the curtain inside, pulled the window together, and pretended I fully closed the window.

Morning came. I felt afraid to look at my sock. I looked and something bulged inside. I grabbed the sock, shoved my hand inside, and yanked out what felt like a doll. A doll! A little brown doll with black curly hair and a soft plush body. The face, a thin plastic that would crack if it fell, looked and felt so fragile. The doll wore a pretty red, yellow, and white striped dress with a bow tied to the back. The hair parted neatly in the middle with two red ribbons tied in ponytails. Excited, I shouted, "Yeeeaah!"

I hugged the doll and galloped to the kitchen where Mama cooked. I stopped at the door.

"Mama, Mama, look!" I said. "Santa Claus brought me this doll."

"You like it?"

"Yes, I prayed last night. That's why Santa brought it for me."

"Just take care of it."

"I'm going to take care of it."

I waited and waited for the next Christmas to come so that I could get something else in my sock.

The next Christmas arrived and after hanging my sock again on the headboard, there was nothing inside in the morning. I told Mama and she asked me if I had asked Santa for another doll. When I told her I didn't, she said that was the reason I didn't get a new doll. The next year she said I didn't pray, that's why I didn't get the Christmas gift I had asked for.

Now, although I hate Mama, I think about the sacrifice she had made to buy the doll for me that year. I now wonder if Shernette or Bridgette received gifts and I wonder if Andrea baked a cake or if John is having a good time here in Kingston. I hope everyone gets a piece of cake.

~~◆~~

Mrs. Bartley gathers food for dinner. Later, Mrs. Bartley and I prepare a big Christmas dinner. Roast chicken and roast beef, ham, rice and peas, potato salad, lettuce mixed with diced tomatoes and shredded carrots with sorrel drink and carrot juice. The house breathes the smell of roasted meat. At the table, we slice tender juicy meat and scoop rice with peas. I chew meat, munch lettuce and sip sorrel. While everyone talks, I think about Hector's River. I miss my friends. I can't help but think about them. They will walk the streets this evening—everyone wearing new clothes. Christmas clothes, sacrifices parents make once a year. Apart from uniforms and school shoes, socks and underwear, some children might not receive any new clothes again until next Christmas.

As the Christmas season rolls away, the New Year rolls in, and in rolls my birthday. Mrs. Bartley asks me if I've ever had a birthday party and I told her no. She tells me she plans for us to celebrate this one. I am glad. Two of the children have birthdays close to mine so we'll have a big birthday celebration. For the party, I invite only one of my school friends, Sandra.

Sandra attends my party and I introduce her to the Bartleys. Mrs. Bartley serves us juice, fruits, cheese, crackers and a big cake with white frosting, sixteen candles and words written in red

Sweet Sixteen

Happy Birthday Peaches

We play songs. The Bartleys and I laugh, chat and joke. Sandra does not say much. She stays close to me. She leaves before night falls. I walk with her to the bus stop.

On Monday, at school, Sandra asks, "Is Mrs. Bartley really your aunt?"

"Of course," I say.

Sandra doesn't have to know I ran away.

"Well, why do you call her Mrs. Bartley and not Aunt Bartley?"

Sandra doesn't have to know I live with strangers who have become my family.

"I don't know." I shrug. "Maybe because I wasn't raised with her and she's not my favorite aunt."

If I say Mrs. Bartley is my aunt, and she's not, what's wrong with that?

"That's strange." Sandra stares at me.

If I want to think or feel Mrs. Bartley is my aunt, then she is. For now.

"That's what we do in my family. Sometimes," I say. "Sometimes I don't say aunt."

I told Sandra when I first met her that I live with the Bartleys because my mother asked them to keep me before she left for Canada. At that time, I told Sandra Mrs. Bartley was my aunt. That's all. I don't know why it matters to Sandra what title I call someone. I'm too ashamed of my past—a fifteen-year-old runaway who had a boyfriend—to divulge anything.

~~ ◆ ~~

February fourteenth arrives. Audition day at Tuff Gong. Since coming to live with the Bartleys, I told myself I would not attend my audition. I'm living a different life. The Bartleys have never said anything bad about Rastafarians, but I don't want to go because I don't want them to know that I had associated myself with Rastafarians or that I wanted to sing a song with reggae beat. And, though Bob Marley sang so many good reggae songs and make reggae music and Jamaica more popular overseas, some Jamaicans still cannot accept reggae because Rastafarians and ganja go together like rice and peas. And since reggae mixes with both, some Jamaicans, especially Christians and some rich people do not like the combination: Rastafarians, reggae, and ganja. Mama is poor and doesn't like Rastafarians. So how can I expect the Bartleys to like me getting mixed-up with ganja-smoking, reggae-singing, and uncombed-hair Rastafarians?

People say many bad things about Rastafarians. There was a rumor that somebody found a forty-leg centipede, in the locks of a Rastafarian. A singer defended the Rastafarian in the song titled "Forty Leg."

People also say that Rastafarians are crazy, that they smoke too much ganja, that they are dirty, and that they go insane when they smoke. Barry, who helped me sing, though he was a Rastafarian, he was never dirty or smelly.

I pass Tuff Gong Studios every day. I travel to school and come home and I wonder what would have happened if I had gone to the audition.

~~ ◆ ~~

Marla walks around the house with a roll of toilet paper and a box of tissue. When she's not sneezing, she's blowing her nose. I think it's such a waste to see her unroll so many pieces of toilet paper and pull so many sheets of tissue from the box. Whenever Mama allowed me to use toilet paper, I had to do so sparingly because we could not afford to buy it. I've heard that people in Russia have to stand in long lines just to buy a roll.

It was such fun when Shernette and I waited for the truck with the Coptic people to drive through Hector's River. The Coptic people in the truck were Rastafarians. They traveled to Hector's River frequently to distribute their newspaper. Pictures of ganja plants spread throughout the paper. The Coptics had their own church, shops, and land. They encouraged ganja smoking but I thanked God each time they arrived.

As we waited by the roadside, two men with long thick locks stood in the back of the truck and they tossed the Coptic newspaper to us. Shernette and I scrambled and pushed between some of our cousins and friends to grab as many newspapers as we could, as if we were excited to read them. The Coptics were happy to see us scramble for the papers and sometimes they threw more. Shernette and I counted to see how many we both collected. I don't know if the Coptic people thought we scrambled for the paper because we wanted to help them spread their news or if they thought we badly wanted to read it. But whatever they thought, the paper came in handy. In piles, Shernette and I lay them on the toilet's floor. A real blessing. Most times I read the paper before I wiped.

"You're not coming from the toilet? Why're you taking so long?" Mama yelled sometimes.

"It can't come out," I hollered back.

Seeing Marla waste precious toilet paper when people in Hector's River still have to use newspaper and old notebooks makes me sad. Such a waste. Marla sits here by the dining room table, minding her own business in her world of sneezing and blowing in toilet paper or tissue. I play with Laura and Nadia and I don't know why Marla doesn't join in our games. I don't understand all about her and the tissue box and toilet paper. So I run, I laugh, and I chase Laura and Nadia. We run under the table and behind the couch. And little Larry kneels on the floor pushing forward and pulling backwards his little car, making his car-playing noises, "Zoooom, zoooom."

Marla sits still on a chair as we run and giggle around her. And then as I'm about to run past her, she rushes before me, charges at me and brings me to a jerky stop. Marla freaks. Her hands fly from her sides and all I can feel is Marla. With her hands like wings flapping, Marla beats on me. My poor breasts have not so long ago recovered and now I might have to worry about them again.

"I hate you. I hate you. I hate you," Marla says in a loud, squeaky voice.

The house falls silent. Laura, Nadia, and Larry stare at us.

"What did I do?"

I cross my chest with my hands and allow her to continue hitting me. I can't hit her back. This is not my house.

"I hate you. I hate you," Marla says. She will not shut up, as if she really wants to rub it into my head. I can't count how many licks I'm getting because Marla seems unable to stop herself. "I hate you. I hate you."

Finally, somebody hates me back. She slows down. She stops. I want to ask Marla, "Are you tired now?" But I don't. This is not my home.

Marla throws herself on her bed. She sobs. She weeps. Shouldn't I be the one crying? I sit on the chair Marla had sat on and cross my arms.

Laura and Nadia walk up to me and Larry brings his car to me and climbs onto my lap. Laura, with her bright, beautiful eyes says, "It's OK."

It happened so fast. I wasn't thinking about feeling sad for myself, but because Laura said that to me and Larry sits on my lap, I feel they feel sorry for me. Now I feel sorry for myself and I can't help thinking about Hector's River. Life was good in Hector's River. It was good even when things were bad. There was a time when Shernette and I fought.

But I can't fight back here. This is not my home. The Bartleys are not my family. Not my blood. Water gathers in my eyes.

"Sorry, Peaches," Nadia says.

I lower my head over my lap to hide my face. Water sprinkles my lap. Laura hands me a tissue.

21
Your Mother Told Me

Water from the tap dribbles over dirty dishes from the dinner we just ate. My mind drifts as I dream that life is not so difficult here in Kingston at the Bartley's house. I guess my mood shifts between loving both places: Kingston and Hector's River. The dishwashing liquid, diluted with water, suds and dissolves down the drain.

"Would you like to visit your mother?" Mrs. Bartley startles me.

Disbelief digs into me as I dilly-dally, unsure what to say. "Uhhnnn, if it's OK with you." I try my best to keep my voice strong to disguise my shock. She has not asked much about Mama. Maybe I'm the only daughter right now who hates her mother and that's something I wouldn't want anyone in my new life to know. I can't let Mrs. Bartley know I had wished never to see Mama again. Now I'll have to pretend that I don't mind seeing Mama because a good daughter could never hate her mother.

"We could visit your mother," she says.

I guess I better say it. "Yes," I say.

"Good. We can go next Sunday. No church."

Sunday comes too fast. I don't know how this trip will turn out. All of us pile into the car and brace ourselves for the fifty-something miles on the country road to Hector's River.

Mrs. Bartley spots some orchids along the side of the road near to Hector's River. The orchids grow wild on the trees. In my mind, as I see them latching onto the trees, I think of the orchids only as parasites. Who would want parasites?

For Mrs. Bartley, orchids are beautiful. Period. She grows them on one side of her yard. For me, I can't see the reason why on earth a plant would want to live on another plant.

"Pull over. Pull over." Mrs. Bartley taps Mr. Bartley on the shoulder.

Mr. Bartley had already flown past the orchids. "We'll see more," he says and he drives slower. More and more orchids, in different spots, latch onto trees and Mr. Bartley parks the car on a straight stretch of road instead of a curve to stay safe. The road to Hector's River winds narrowly. And drivers drive deadly crazy there.

I can't believe these two people. The Bartleys stretch their arms and break orchids from their lifelines. Mama and I perform smiles to put on a show for the Bartleys as I walk from the car. My smile is as fake as fake can be. But I know Mama's smile is real.

~~ ◆ ~~

A neighbor watches and Mama yells to her, "She's here."

Probably she is proud that I'm not pregnant and that I live with a good family. Mama's face shows she has lost a few pounds. Now she's about one hundred and thirty to one hundred and forty. I, on the other hand, have gained fifteen pounds.

It's hard for me to hide my feelings. I do not run to Mama and do not pretend as if I'm excited to see her. I talk to the girls, stare at the sea, and tell the girls how powerful and beautiful the sea in Hector's River is. I hug Bridgette and say hi to Shernette, who knows I really don't care about talking to her. She tries, saying, "How are you?" "How is Kingston?" and for all her questions, I reply, "OK." "OK." I don't know why I still feel mad and angry with Shernette. I wonder if it's because running away wasn't something that I had aspired to do.

Mama asks how I'm doing, I say "OK," and I see a sad stare coming from her eyes, as if saying, "I've lost my daughter." And even with that stare, there's a stare of contentment, as if it say that she's happy that I'm well. I don't know why I feel uncomfortable talking to her. Maybe it's because I'm embarrassed about what I did, how I left, stealing her money. Thank God Mr. Isaac is not around; he's probably at work. Mama had prepared Kool-Aid for us drink, and after drinking, I leave her to talk with the Bartleys.

I tell the girls to come with me to the sea, anything to take me from Mama's presence, to take me from the uneasy feelings. I hold Bridgette's hand as she walks with us. I look behind me and see Shernette running to follow us. I keep walking.

We stand on a cliff beside the sea. On one side, I show the children the depth of the water and tell them that sharks like it there. I tell them that a drop of blood would bring the sharks in sight and that they gathered there when people threw dead animals over the cliff. The children marvel at how the waves crash against the rocks and splash high in the air like sea spouts. Once, John and some other boys jumped over this cliff for the fun of doing so and Shernette and I ran to tell Mama who said she would give John a beating, but she didn't.

On the other side of the cliff, I lead the children down a little path to the seashore. I show off the pretty rocks and the seashells. They stick their toes into the water feeling its warmth. They say, "Oh. Nice!" And I want them to see that I had things right where I lived in Hector's River that they do not have where they live in Kingston.

I take the girls with me to show them one of my friends. I run to see Andrea too. And as I arrive back to Mama, I see her talking with Mrs. Bartley and nothing as far as I can see tells me that Mama is not talking about me. My jolly mood sinks somewhere inside me. Mrs. Bartley just keeps shaking and nodding her head and Mr. Bartley sits on the veranda, reading as usual. I walk back into the yard and pass Mama and Mrs. Bartley.

Before we leave, Mama gives us coconut jelly that we put into the car trunk. I barely open my mouth to say goodbye to Mama. I'm ashamed about all that happened between the two of us.

~~♦~~

We set off back to Kingston to get home before night meets us on the road. I still can't find any space in my heart to love Mama. Not yet. In Kingston, when Mr. Bartley sleeps and the children lie in their beds, Mrs. Bartley approaches me.

"I want to talk to you," she says.

I smile. In the kitchen where no one can hear us, I stand against the counter. Mrs. Bartley stands before me. The light from the light bulb shines brightly. The tap next to me drips. Drips. I turn the tap tightly. The house sits quiet. We stare at each other. I tense. My stomach knots.

"Your mother told me," Mrs. Bartley says slowly.

I look down at my fingers playing with each other. Please, not my secret, I think.

"Look at me."

I raise my head and seal my lips.

"She told me everything."

I wish she would just tell me fast or don't tell me at all. This is so painful. My heart won't slow its beats.

"You had a boyfriend."

My knees shake. They always shake when I'm nervous. And if I sit, they will shake harder, and I really won't know that they are shaking or that I'm even nervous. Mrs. Bartley always reminded me not to shake them.

"She said you ran away."

I hate Mama more.

Mrs. Bartley says she will not tell her husband. "I'll keep it a secret," she says.

"Thank you," I say and smile. I feel the knots untie a little in my stomach. But shame takes over my mind. I don't think I've ever felt so uncomfortable as I am feeling now. I don't know how I can look at

Mrs. Bartley tomorrow. But I love and thank her in my heart for not telling the children or Mr. Bartley. I thank her for not sending me back home.

On my bed, I close my eyes, but sleep will not come. I turn from my back to my side. I turn and turn until I sleep.

In the morning, I wake up early, make breakfast, and head to school. At school, all morning I think about what Mrs. Bartley knows about me. My secret is exposed. I don't feel the same when I'm around her. I've been bad, I ran away, I had a boyfriend, and I stole money. I want to hide myself. After school I head home. After changing my clothes, I cook dinner. When the Bartleys' car turns into the driveway, I rush to the bedroom and open my schoolbooks. I pretend to do my homework.

~~ ◆ ~~

I don't know if it's the visit to see Mama that changed my relationship with Mrs. Bartley or the discovery of my secret. But I don't feel the same way at the Bartleys' home as I did before. Days seem long and work seems burdensome. Mrs. Bartley tries to make me put curlers in her hair one evening and I thought that my duties were already enough.

"Peaches, can you put some rollers in my hair?" Mrs. Bartley asks.

I pause before I answer. I could tell Mama, I'm tired. I could tell Mama, later. I can't with Mrs. Bartley. I do everything she says because she has been good to me.

"I've never put curlers in anybody's hair," I lie.

"I'll show you how," she says. Mrs. Bartley takes a section of hair and wraps it around the curler. "See, easy."

Of course, I say to myself, to embark to do the worst job I will have ever done the best way I can. I take the curler and pretend to twist Mrs. Bartley's hair loosely around it and then let go. Each time I let go, the curler falls from her hair onto the floor.

"Like this." Mrs. Bartley demonstrates again how to put the curler in her hair. If she can do it, I think, why doesn't she?

"It's not working," I say.

The curlers fall on the floor.

"Just like this."

"Oh, oh. It's not working."

The curlers fall on the floor.

"OK, I'll do it," Mrs. Bartley says after my four attempts with the curlers landing always on the floor.

I celebrate inside.

I feel I don't belong. If I had somewhere else to go, I'd take off. I feel dirty and sinful, not pure any more. She knows who I was and who I am. I'm not the nice girl she believed.

I don't like to go out on Sundays with the Bartleys any more. I'm getting older—almost seventeen—and the Bartleys want me to stroll behind them and the kids as if I were still fifteen. I don't mind staying home alone. I love loneliness. I love my own sorrow. It comforts me.

One Sunday. "We're going to the beach," Mrs. Bartley announces.

"I don't want to come."

Another Sunday. "We are going to visit…."

"I don't want to come." I do the same every week.

We talk less. We talk just a tiny bit. I just do my housework. I talk only to the children.

At school, however, I shine. It's now September, the beginning of a new school year and my grade eleven classmates all vote for me to be the class prefect. Imagine me the fornicator, the runaway, the thief, and the liar, now I'm the leader of the class. If my classmates only knew more about me they would not have put me in this high position. Every school day I wear my little pin with the word PREFECT on it. My classmates respect me. I don't respect myself.

Three weeks before the Christmas break from school, Sandra tells me she will go home to the village where she's from for the holidays. Mrs. Bartley had mentioned to me that my cousin, Vanessa, informed her that Mama is visiting Canada. After learning that Sandra will be away and because Mama is in Canada, I want to take advantage of Mama's absence. I miss my own family. I miss Andrea and Bridgette.

"Can I talk to you?" I say to Mrs. Bartley before to I go to sleep.

"Sure," she says.

"Can I go home for Christmas?"

Mrs. Bartley pauses. She stares at me and I wonder what she thinks.

"Sure," she says. Mrs. Bartley turns as she walks away.

"Thanks," I say. I am happy. I could have never guessed that Mrs. Bartley would have said yes so easily, so instantly.

Mrs. Bartley turns around. She stares at me.

"Take all your stuff. Pack everything."

Mrs. Bartley responds calmly as if she had long ago planned her words. "Pack everything."

I cannot hold back my tears. They gush. I know what "pack everything" means. Goodbye. Leave. Go away. Stay away. Don't come back. I stand still, not knowing how to move, what to say, what to do. She says nothing more to me.

I cry as I break the news to Nadia in the evening. I cry as I lie on the bed in the night thinking of all that I have done wrong that maybe led to my banishment. I cry as I make breakfast in the kitchen in the morning and I think about all my sins, ruining the book, not liking Marla as I should and not wanting to go out with the Bartleys any more. I cry after returning from school, I play "Chiquitita," and I cry and cry. My fifteen-year-old strength, anger, and bravery are all gone. I must return home as the prodigal son in the Bible. I wish I had not asked to go to Hector's River.

What will I do in Hector's River? What will become of me?

No more school. Only six months to go. I'm doing well. The teacher likes me. My friends like me, even Paul, although I haven't spoken to him since the time he threatened me with the penknife. My sins, the lies, stealing from and dishonoring my mother have come back to haunt me. I can't cry at school or tell my real story to get some pity from anyone. The story I tell is a happy one or should be. With a straight face, I tell my teacher that Mama will return from Canada and that I will have to go back home and won't come back in January. I tell the same thing to Sandra. We exchange addresses.

I can't stop thinking about the reasons the Bartleys want to get rid of me just like that. Maybe Mrs. Bartley found *The Joy of Sex* and she saw how I destroyed it after invading her privacy. She thinks I'm evil. Maybe she doesn't want me around her kids any more. I may influence them. Maybe she doesn't know what to do with me after I graduate. What to do with a runaway if I don't have a job? Maybe she thinks it's just time for me to return home. Maybe she wants Mama to take back her daughter. Maybe she waited for the right time, the time she thought I was ready to go back. Maybe. Maybe. Maybe.

The night before I leave, Mrs. Bartley hands me a book for my Christmas present. Although I'm supposed to wait for Christmas to open it, I don't. On the top of the bunk, before I sleep, I secretly and quietly tear away the wrapper. The title startles me, *How to Uplift the Burdens That Weigh You Down.* I remember when Mrs. Bartley bought it on a ship that had docked downtown at the wharf. I was with her. I thought she had bought the book for herself.

I don't know what Mrs. Bartley is thinking about, I had never consciously thought about my troubles, past and present, as burdens, but I guess they are. The secrets and shame, they are burdens. Hating my mother, that is a burden. Living a lie, that is a burden.

Sometimes other people have to let us know that we carry burdens. Bottom Church members used to say, "Take your burdens to the Lord." But at thirteen, fourteen and fifteen, that was just a meaningless phrase, words I responded to without knowledge. I understand. Now I do.

A few days before Christmas, the Bartleys nicely and politely leave me with my big luggage at the bus station where all the vehicles going to the countryside park. They leave me here with a new burden. It's the burden of going back home.

How does a runaway feel or should feel when she goes back home? What do I tell people why I can't go back to Kingston to complete the last six months of my secondary education? What story do I tell? Well, maybe that's why I have the book. To help me with these burdensome questions.

"Goodbye." The Bartleys say, "Goodbye."

I plan a new lie, a new answer to questions people will ask.

22
Like Strangers

I won't come home to an empty house to play music and dance and cry. Maybe going back home is good for me. Mrs. Bartley did her part. She helped when I needed help. She taught me so much about life without saying a word about life to me. I learned about rich and poor people. I learned about family, that there are different kinds and that families do different things. I learned that parents could raise good children without ever spanking them.

~~ ◆ ~~

I wonder how the number fifteen could cause so much pain—all that happened when I turned fifteen. It's not even the fact that so much is happening in Jamaica and all over the world, like the shooting of Pope John Paul II, the death of Bob Marley by cancer, the war between Iran and Iraq—I didn't even know about those countries whose last letters change the pronunciation of their names until I heard on

BBC Radio that Iraq attacked Iran and now they are fighting. All over Jamaica, there are food shortages and some food storeowners marry one type of food with another food for sale—rice with peas and flour with sugar. Some food items do not even go with each other. I don't know how flour works with sugar unless you need both for baking.

Now Jamaica has two cities, Kingston and Montego Bay. This happened in May. What's great is that the new Prime Minister, Edward Seaga, has severed diplomatic ties with Cuba. That's what I heard on BBC Radio too. Thank God. When I was younger, I used to have nightmares that Jamaica would become like Cuba that is so close to Jamaica and that other countries like the United States would be mad at us, especially if we talk with the Russians, too, and we would starve because people would have to share everything they have even if those things are not enough to share. I heard that our former Prime Minister, Michael Manley, would take away people's rights, that children would starve, that the Government would spy on everyone and everything everybody does, that no one could talk anything bad about the government, and that no one could leave Jamaica as freely as they want to. Well that's what some of the adults said would happen if Michael Manley made Jamaica into a communist country. Because we didn't have much of anything to share, I remember that Mama's worry was that she wouldn't leave Jamaica.

Now that I have to go back to Hector's River, I'm ready to try to handle the burdens.

The smell of the salty sea greets me as I step off the bus in Hector's River. I lumber to the house and drop my suitcase—the brown one Mrs. Bartley gave me—on the floor. Before Mama went to visit Rose in Canada, she moved next door to Mr. Isaac's house. He sort-of watches over Shernette and Bridgette. I hope Mr. Isaac doesn't think he should watch over me too because I'm almost seventeen. Shernette and I talk but I'm still a bit uncomfortable around her.

By the time I settle, Robert moves swiftly back into my life. With Mama not here, and living all the way in Canada, Robert and I see each other freely. I can see Andrea and Raquel too.

Mama returns and I feel the tension, the strangeness between us. I still hate her, not as much, though. Mama has brought clothes, shoes, and underwear from Canada. She sorts out piles of clothes for each one of us. Ungratefully, I seize what she gives me, but I do not say much to her.

The next day I meet Andrea to give her some clothes Mama brought for her. We haven't discussed anything about Mama as I feel we both share a mutual feeling of hate for our mother.

"She said I should give you these," I pass the items to Andrea. And as she reaches to take the bag from me, I say, "I hate her."

"What?" Andrea pops out her eyes.

I wonder why she reacted like that. For all I know, the last time I talked with Andrea, she didn't say anything about Mama. I've been thinking that she hates Mama almost as much as I do.

"What happened?" I say.

"Mama is good." Andrea stares hard and cold at me. "She's a good woman," Andrea says again.

"Andrea, I didn't say she's not good."

"She's good. She's not bad."

I recoil. Shock. This is not the Andrea I knew before I left Hector's River. What happened to her when I was away? Did Andrea fall back in love with Mama? Now I'm alone in the land of hatred. How can I forgive Mama? Or pretend nothing happened? How do I love her again?

My heart wants to keep hating Mama, but with Andrea not on my side and even as stubborn as I am, I'll have to find a way to love Mama again. I can't be a lone hater.

The next day Mama tells Shernette and me that she has good news for us. "I wanted to wait," Mama says. "But I can't keep it any more."

Naturally, I want to know the good news and a big smile takes over my face.

"We're going to Canada," Mama says. "Rose and her husband are sponsoring all of us."

It's like a dream. Canada, Canada, Canada is all I can hear in my head.

"Yeah!" Shernette and I shout. We hardly ever fight now and we're closer to each other. Bridgette copies us.

"All of us?" I ask.

"Well, Andrea and John can't come because the two of them are over twenty-one, plus Andrea is married. Immigration law won't allow them."

I guess Mama will lose two of her children and regain the two older ones—Jason and Rose who live in Canada. Mr. Isaac stays in Jamaica too because he's not married to Mama. I feel good, but I'm sad that Andrea and John won't be able to come to Canada with us. I guess it's not hard to hate Mama if she's good to me. I like her a little.

With Mama around, Robert and I hide when we meet.

"The two of you still together?" Mama says. I know she means Robert and me.

"Yes," I say in a shy voice.

"Tell him I want to meet him."

"OK."

I just can't believe all the good news I've been hearing. Mama is really making me forget about hate. I like Mama more. Meet Robert? I deliver the good news to Robert and he's glad and arranges to meet with Mama the next day. At the meeting, Robert and Mama talk.

"Why do you want to be with her?" Mama says.

"I don't really know, Miss. I just know that I really love her."

"You know what love is?"

"I know what love is. I know I love Peaches the first time I saw her."

"So you plan to marry her someday?" Mama says.

"Yes, Miss."

I blush, twirl my fingers, wriggle my toes, and smile.

"You must respect her and be good to her," Mama says.

"Yes, Miss."

Robert and Mama talk and shake hands and for the first time, I walk with Robert in her presence. We walk together to the end of the lane and I feel so proud of Mama. Something stirs in my heart for her. She's good. I need to love her more.

June arrives. Students dressed in fancy clothes for their graduation, pass the laneway near Mama's house. Ashamed, I run to the house to hide. I cry. My former high school friends are graduating, but not me. I am the one who did everything wrong and did not complete high school. I cry for my missed graduation. I'm ashamed of myself. I don't have a job. Where will I find one without a high school education? Here or in Kingston, I would have graduated if I had been good. I would have a job.

As I cry, someone raps hard at the door, and Shernette opens it, and I hear Raquel's voice.

"Peaches here?"

I quickly wipe my face and shout, "Tell her I'm coming."

Raquel stands in the middle sporting a fancy dress and wearing high heels.

"Check me out," she says with a big smile on her face.

"Looking good," I say.

"Graduation was good."

"Can imagine," I say.

"Let's go for a walk."

"I'm tired." I do not want the other students to see me.

"Come on. We can dance at the bar."

"You need to go home and take off those heels or else your feet are going to bawl tonight."

"I know how to walk in them." Raquel lifts one foot and stares at the heel of her shoe.

"I'm just tired, Raquel. Did too much today."

"Alright." She walks away. "You're missing a good party."

"Dance for me." I cry inside as I wave goodbye.

23
Policemen

A team of runners and high and long jumpers from Hector's River sets out to Port Antonio early one Saturday morning to meet other teams and compete. Since Mama gave me license to be with Robert, I board the bus with him. Our first public journey together and we sit side by side.

During the games, Robert and I share snacks and lunch and we stay with each other like conjoined twins. After the games, we sit side by side in the bus and wait for it to leave. Then, a girl, nicely shaped, wanders pass the window. Immediately, Robert seems to have forgotten I sit beside him. He dives before me, cranes his neck, and pushes his head out the window.

"Hey! Pretty girl," he hollers.

I'm still trying to wrestle with what Robert just did and as he motions the girl to come by the window. The girl shakes her head and wanders on. Robert retreats back to his upright position beside me and I cross my arms and sit silently. Robert begs for my forgiveness.

Leaving the bus, I say, "Don't ever talk to me again."

"I'll see you later," Robert says.

At night, I stay inside and read my Bible. I don't need Robert to disrespect me. I want to go back to church. It was safe being there. I was happy there and my thoughts were clean. I didn't have troubles. If I become a Christian again, I can be good again and forget about Robert. The Bible, Ecclesiastics 26:8 states that, "*A jealous woman is the grief and mourning of the heart.*" I don't want grief.

Shernette and Andrea are both Christians now and I should join them. I go to church with them the next night. The church members are glad to have me back and they want me to accept God in my life again. I might even get baptized again to rid me of all the sins—too many to count—that I've committed over the last two years.

I feel the connection to God again, especially when I'm in church and hear the members as they praise God and bellow from the depths of their souls. It's nice to have such a connection with God. What else could people ask for when they have so much joy? Thanks to the Bible that I'm now reading every day, I think about God instead of Robert.

But it's hard to keep Robert from me. As I stroll home one day, I notice Robert sitting, waiting for me on the wall I don't like, the low wall where the men sit and talk and observe all the people passing by. As I near Robert, he walks beside me. I keep walking.

"I'm sorry," Robert says. "How many times do you want me to tell you? Just talk to me."

"No."

I'm not as strong as I want to be. We connect again. Robert and I meet this night and he babbles about how strong he is and about how women like when men slap them. I don't know how this conversation started about men hitting women.

"I can slap you," he says.

"No you can't."

"Yes I can."

"You can't."

"Oh yeah, I can hit you hard."

"You can't hit me."

"I can." Robert points at me.

"You can't. I'm not joking."

"Don't push me."

"What's wrong with you? You can't hit me. Why do you want to hit me?"

I turn and look into the darkness and stare at Robert as he grabs my hand.

"Let me go."

"I can hit you." Robert grins.

He seems serious. I know I must get out of this. I don't know why he's acting this way. He's never hit me before. I try to walk away, but Robert pulls my hand and before I try to pull away again, Robert's palm, hard, slams against the thin skin that covers the bone in my jaw. Bells ring in my ears. Shock freezes me. I see a dark sky and bright stars. No one can hear my night cries. I bolt through the dark, unafraid.

Robert runs behind me and pulls my dress and his pulling slows my speed. He grabs my hand. "Sorry," Robert says. "I was just testing you."

"I don't care. Don't talk to me." I try to wrestle my hands from his.

"Come on. Peaches. Sorry. You can't take a joke."

"I don't want to talk to you ever again. Let me go." I try to free my hand. "Let me go."

"Sorry. Sorry." He tries to hug me. "It's a joke."

"No man will ever hit me."

I twist and push. There is no point in me trying to resist Robert's hold. I know all too well, the more I do it, the more he will hold on. So I relax and pretend to forgive him.

"I want to go home," I say.

Robert follows me to the dark laneway and watches me walk up to the gate. I lock the gate behind me knowing that this night—the first time Robert slapped me—is the last time, which marks the end of our relationship. I did not agree to be his boxing partner or his punching bag. I will not let a man hit me and stay with him. I will not become what Mama used to be with my Papa or Andrea with Steve.

Mama left Papa. It took a while for her to make that decision. But she left Papa.

I was the youngest of six children, four girls and two boys Mama had before she left Papa. At the time of the move, Rose was eleven, Andrea was ten, Shernette was six, and I was three. Jason was sixteen and John was seven.

Papa drank a lot. Sometimes, after drinking, like an unstable lump of clay, he staggered from the rum shop, bounced against people, tumbled on pavements, zigzagged along the sidewalk and stumbled into the house.

Papa fought Mama whenever he was drunk. The sound of their voices bellowed from the house as they panted angry breaths, and groaned like weary wrestlers, and banged steel pots, and crashed porcelain saucers against the wooden house frame.

The familiar noise escaped the house and brought nosy neighbors in the lane. They peeked through holes and pressed their ears against the used-to-be rusty zinc roof strips that fenced our yard.

Mama didn't like to fight with Papa. She moved out many times but moved back in when she didn't have money or when Papa pleaded with her to come back. He told her sorry. He said he wouldn't hit her again. But he continued to do so.

One Saturday morning, as Papa slept, two policemen walked into our yard and shortly after, an open-back truck arrived with three men and a driver. The truck peeked over the dilapidated fence. The three men helped to carry furniture from the house to the truck as the policemen guarded Mama.

Papa awoke. He surveyed the room. He stared at the two policemen. Shock covered his face

"What's going on?" Papa said.

No one answered. Papa stared as if confused while the men continued taking items from the house to the truck.

Then, after taking the items she wanted, Mama realized that she had forgotten one of her favorite pots. She dashed back into the house. Papa jumped out of bed, scurried to the kitchen, grabbed onto the pot, and tried to pry it from Mama's grip.

Mama and Papa struggled for the pot.

One of the policemen told Mama to leave the pot with Papa.

In the Saturday morning sun, Papa's golden complexion glowed. With hair of big black curls, ruffled from drunken sleep, Papa stared at the big truck waiting, his children leaving, the police officers guarding, and Mama parting.

Papa stood in the kitchen's doorframe, head bowed, barefooted, wearing boxer shorts. One hand rested on his head and the other held the doorframe. In my mind, he whispered in a sad low tone, "Sorry."

For more than two hours, we rode from Kingston to Hector's River in the back of the truck to live with Mama's mother and father. In our new home, some of us slept on the floor while some slept on the one bed Mama carried from Kingston.

Mama shielded us from that world, where it now seems as though Robert wants to take me to. I will not go there.

I did get warnings from words Robert had said and things he had done. But I ignored them as confusion about love impaired my judgment about what was right or wrong.

Earlier on in our relationship, before I ran away, once when we had a disagreement, Robert said I had "dragon jaw bones." I cried because I knew he wanted to hurt my feelings about myself. It worked. At nights I prayed and asked God to flatten the bones in my jaw. I tried to braid my hair to cover my "jaw bones," to give my face a narrow appearance. It was only when I went to Kingston, I accepted my face again. My teacher told me that I had lovely "cheek bones." She said I could be a model. I loved my teacher for saying that to me. I felt better about myself.

A few months ago, too, Robert bragged to me that he slept with someone I knew. Then he said sorry.

Once, when I didn't want to talk to him, he said I had pimples and that God knew why he gave them to me. I hated my face with all the pimples.

Robert said sorry. But I know that sorry is a word with no meaning. I think I know when it's time to quit something bad. The words were said, the actions were taken, the warning is now clear. This is not the person I want in my life. This is not the husband I want. "When you feel, you will learn." I understand your words, Mama. I understand.

~ ~ ◆ ~ ~

Faint, swollen fingerprints redden my jaw up to my ears as I glance into the mirror the next morning. I braid my hair and let the braids cover the fingerprints. I can't afford to let Shernette or Mama see them. I had vowed on my bed, in the night, that I'll go back to church and forget about Robert. I no longer want to talk to boys. Each day when I go to the store and when I go to church at nights, I travel with someone Robert does not like or someone who does not like him. I travel with Shernette most of the time. Robert stays away. He calls to me, but does not come near. I've told Shernette I'm no longer going out with Robert.

The clear sky hovers cloudless, the sweltering road stretches endlessly.

Three weeks later, to my surprise, on my way back home, with Mama walking beside me in the afternoon heat, Robert walks up behind us. I look at him and I ignore him. Robert calls to me with his finger. I ignore him. He greets Mama and then says, "Peaches, I want to talk to you."

"Got nothing to say to you."

"Talk to your daughter, please," Robert says to Mama.

Mama says nothing.

Mama and I walk on, ignoring Robert. The more we ignore him, the more he speaks words that are not nice.

Then, in a strong and angry voice, he blurts, "You're a No Nation."

People use this phrase when they want to insult someone about heritage, race or class.

"What?" I cast an angry look at him.

"No Nation," Robert says again. "Miss, talk to your daughter, please."

"Oh Lord," Mama says in frustration. "Give us some peace," she orders Robert.

"I just want to talk to her."

"She doesn't want to talk to you," Mama says. "You mustn't force people to do what they don't want to do."

"I won't talk to you. Ever again," I say.

Robert continues to trail behind us, walking as if we were pulling him by a string. He grabs my wrist, stares and pleads with his eyes.

"I just want to talk you. Listen to me." He jerks my hand.

"No," I say, still holding on to Mama's hand. "Let me go."

Robert releases my hand and trails behind us. He curses, saying everything possible to get us mad. Mama and I pretend we can't hear him and he slows his pace, stops and turns around.

Long ago, Mama knew I was too young to take on the burdens of living as an adult. People say that with age comes wisdom. If I could live my life all over, I would listen to Mama, though I'm glad that I went to Kingston, saw a different kind of life, and learned many different things that I may have never learned had I stayed in Hector's River.

Mama and I stroll over the hill. We drift further and further from Robert.

I hope this is the end of him with me.

24
Mama Feels Happy

The sky arches and spreads like an immense pale-grey carpet, camouflaging its separation from the sea, shedding water everywhere. We—Mama, Shernette, Bridgette, and I remove everything from outside, everything we do not want the rain to wet. I'm sure men in Hector's River will go crab hunting tonight, to grab crabs seeking night food or those running from their holes, afraid their shelter will cave in on them.

Thunder claps and rumbles, fading in the distance. The May rain beats on our zinc rooftop and like a tranquilizer, it soothes my mind. It blows toward the front of our house. It strikes against the windowpanes. It smacks banana and mango trees. It rests on the leaves, forms tiny bubbles that roll from the leaves and splatter on the ground. It soaks the parched earth. It pools in little streams and trickles from the yard and runs into the laneway. Leaves sag. Animals stay still. People shelter in their homes.

Under the mango tree in the front yard, jittery yellow baby chickens cluster beneath their mother as she braves the weather. They push each other up and under her wings, between her legs and among her feathers as she hunches quietly with her head lowered and her eyes closed. The rain soaks the mother.

Under the wooden seat near the mango tree, our four dogs bob their heads with their mouths open and their tongues hanging. They seek shelter from the rain, still in solidarity, still steadfast, still silently guarding the house.

Under our zinc roof, Mama feels happy. That's all that matters. That's all that should matter. We huddle on her bed, happy that our time to leave Jamaica is near. Mama reaches for our passports. Love flows from her eyes. I see it.

Mama loves us. She loves me. Why did I do that to her? Why did I hate her with such intensity? How did I become such monster who hated my own blood, the blood that gave me strength, that runs through every part of my body, that gave me life?

I'm sorry I gave her heartache, shame, and grief. When I left, she must have cried, cried at nights though in the day she must have laughed as she pretended all was well.

From the day I was born, she loved me. When I travelled to work with her, before I started elementary school, we developed a stronger bond as she held my hand and we walked on an unpaved dirt road that soared and led us over a big dirt hill. Stones popped their heads out of the earth.

"Be careful how you walk on these stones," Mama said. "These stones here will mash up any good pair of shoes."

"Yeah, Mama," I said.

Hollow and narrow, small rain-carved tracks twisted between the dirt and stones. The rain-tracks led to the bottom of the hill or into yards.

Mama worked for Mr. and Mrs. Jones. When Mama and I arrived at the top of the hill, one of the highest hills in Hector's River, we turned into the big yard with the big concrete house with the big veranda that welcomed us. Mr. and Mrs. Jones had children living in the house: one son, Edward, and three daughters. The Jones' family was always friendly. They greeted us. Later, Edward fell in love with Rose, and when he immigrated to Canada, he sponsored Rose to live with him, and they got married, and they sponsored Mama to live in Canada too, and that's how Mama and some of her children, including me, now have the opportunity to leave Jamaica.

Mama dumped the dirty clothes under a big tree in the cool shade at the back of the Jones' yard. She put a cloth over two cement blocks and sat on them. Before Mama sat two big aluminum wash pans: one wash pan for clothes not too dirty and one for badly soiled clothes. Beside each wash pan, a basin rested. Sometimes Mama threw clothes in the basin that she thought should not go into the big wash pans. Bundles of clothes spread on the grass. I brought little pails of water to refill the wash pans when the water was not enough to soak the clothes.

"Don't bring so much water," Mama said. "You will strain yourself. Just bring what you can manage."

"OK," I giggled. "But I want to help."

Mama scrubbed clothes and sweat dribbled down her face. I liked the sound her hands made when she washed the clothes. I liked the melody: scrip-scrip, scrip-scrip-scrip, and scrip-scrip. Clothes soaked with suds and water between her hands gave off this musical sound. Some people said that the sound came from people who "washed good." I wanted to wash like Mama.

"Can I try?"

"No, you're going to set me back. I don't want to stay here all day. Another day."

"I am trying hard with all of you. I don't want anyone of you to beg or steal. I just want the best for you."

"Mama, I wouldn't steal."

"I know that."

"Mama, I don't beg nobody nothing. Even when Aunt Patty gives me food sometimes, I tell her I'm not hungry. She said I don't eat from her."

"But you can eat from your auntie. Nothing is wrong with that."

"But I don't want her to think that I'm always hungry."

"That's true. Good. I don't want to hear that any of my children beg anything. It's me alone and I'm trying my best to make all of you turn out to be somebody."

"Where's Papa, Mama?"

"Don't talk about him."

Mama didn't like to talk much about my father. "Is just me," she said every time I asked. I still asked her even though I knew what she would say. The days I stayed at work with Mama were times we grew closer to each other. They were our best moments. I liked when she talked.

"You know you barely made it in this world. If it wasn't for Bev, you wouldn't be here. I would surely have had that abortion because I know I couldn't take care of another child."

"Who's Bev?"

"My friend."

"But it wouldn't matter to me, Mama. If I wasn't born. Well if I wasn't born, I think I wouldn't know anything. I would just be like an invisible person. Right?"

"I'm glad you're here anyway. I'm glad that my friend, Bev, stopped me."

"Me too."

Mama sang gospel songs. I learned them all. She told me stories. Some stories made me laugh until my belly hurt. Some stories about Brer Anansi, the trickster-spider-man, made me laugh harder. Sometimes I ran a few yards from where Mama washed to pick up ripe mangoes that fell from the mango tree. I washed the mangoes and saved a small mango for Mama. I pushed it into her mouth while she washed. I liked when she tried to talk with the mango in her mouth because she talked in gibberish. I mimicked her and laughed. I put a small mango in my mouth and mumbled like Mama.

After work, Mrs. Jones gave Mama a container of cooked food. Mama carried it home and like a mother bird, Mama dipped and scooped food from the container, passing the spoon from mouth to mouth— she fed us all. After passing several spoons to all of us, Mama took the rest for herself—less than she gave us.

~~◆~~

Sometimes Mama and I took our shower together and we readied ourselves for bed. Sometimes, while in bed, Mama played with Shernette and me. We played bicycle—not real bicycle because we had none—we played bicycle with feet against feet, my tiny feet against Mama's as we played on the bed, our heads in opposite directions. We pedaled our feet as though we were riding a bicycle. Whoever grew tired first lost the game. As my feet grew tired, Mama knew.

"My feet are tired," Mama said before I said mine were tired. "You win again."

"I win." I giggled. "I win. Yeaaaah!"

Mama giggled too, turned to Shernette, and played the same game, and she lost again.

~~ ♦ ~~

Mama taught me how to read, making me read the Bible at nights, correcting me when I didn't pronounce the words correctly.

"Wrong," she said.

I chuckled. "How'd you know I said it wrong?"

I wondered how Mama knew I had said the words wrong when she did not look at them.

"Cause I know the words," Mama said.

I laughed and said, "That's funny, Mama, you know many things. You know everything."

Why did I hurt Mama? It was Mama who took care of when the man walked through the window in the night and entered my room. It was her name I called out—the name so powerful that when I cried "Mama," he ran. And she played the doctor, inspected me to make sure I was not hurt. And she took me to the police station to report the incident. She stood with me to wait on the bus to get to court for the trial. She told me as we waited that I should tell the Judge the truth. She sat beside me in the courtroom and provided her shoulder and her arm for me to lean on. She hugged me when I walked from the place where I testified. She comforted me at nights when I had bad dreams and tried to shield me from the memory so I could forget what had happened and I hid the memory for years. I can't believe that I hated Mama.

Mama checks and rechecks and counts and recounts the passports she hides in her room in a compartment on the headboard of her bed. Six more months she counts down. Five more months. If Mama didn't talk like a sane woman, I would certainly think she's going crazy. I don't know if she thinks someone will snatch the passports from the headboard.

At fifteen, I didn't believe her promise that we would leave Jamaica. I don't know if she believed it when she said it. So much distance separated us—our understanding about each other, what we expected from each other—my anger and hate. One day, not now, I must learn the truth about the night when she beat me.

"This is mine, this is yours," she flashes our passport pictures. "Shernette and Bridgette." She places the passports on the bed where I sit beside her. "All of them here."

"Ugh, I hate my picture," I say.

"It's you," Mama says.

She stares at me.

We laugh.

"It looks uglier than me."

"Still your picture."

"Don't like it."

"You have to like you."

"Don't want to see it."

I grab Mama's passport and stare at her picture.

"Yours look better."

"It's just a picture," Mama says and smiles.

"It's still you."

Mama takes the passport from me. She gathers the rest, mine, Shernette's and Bridgette's, and binds them with an elastic band.

"Two more months," Mama says.

"Time will fly. Fast." I look out the window.

The rain pitter-patters now. The thunder rumbles softly far away. The sky peers brighter over the land.

"The rain is easing up," I say. I stare at Mama. "Look, just drizzle."

I pull back the curtains that block the window. The rain falls lightly.

~~◆~~

A few minutes before we leave Hector's River to get to the airport, we pose for a picture: Mama, Andrea, John, Shernette, Bridgette, and me. I hope God will take care of Andrea and John.

Standing on the side of the street, we hold hands while Andrea says a prayer. Her request to God is to guide, protect, and keep us safe at all times, and to make us remember him in good and bad times. The prayer ends with an "Amen" from everyone. Andrea's unselfish prayer was for the ones leaving, not the ones staying behind. Mama's two children who went to live in Kingston, what will happen to them? Will they ever see Canada?

PART THREE
ACROSS THE SEA

25
Talent for Self-torture

Tears roll down our faces as we hug and say goodbye to a crying Andrea, a quiet John, and a sad Mr. Isaac at Norman Manley International Airport in Kingston.

When we board the airplane, a flight attendant escorts Shernette, Bridgette and me to see the pilot. I just can't believe that I'm on a plane and I'm seeing a pilot for the first time in my life.

The plane glides over Pearson International Airport, Toronto, Canada. The city that lights up like cities I've only seen on postcards. As we leave the airport, a different kind of cool July breeze reminds me that I'm no longer in Jamaica. Rose meets and greets us at the airport and takes us to the apartment where she lives with her husband, Edward, and two young daughters.

This apartment is now a "full house," but for this family, this is a happy home. It's four plus four, making eight of us. Edward welcomes us with his usual sincere smile and warm hugs. There is food galore, everywhere in the kitchen. Over and over, Mama says, "God bless Rose and her husband."

~~ ◆ ~~

Life in Canada is good. Soon, a neighbor gets a job for Mama in a factory. Shernette gets a job in a factory too. Now, September, Bridgette goes to school. On Sundays, I attend church and on weekdays I attend high school again. All the students in my class are younger. There's just so much to get used to: the students, many Whites, and a handful of Blacks. The students do strange things that I would not have done in Jamaica. In the girls' restroom, the girls pee loudly while I try to squeeze my pee. Aren't decent girls supposed to urinate discreetly?

For gym, the girls change their clothes in the locker room before and after gym class and I can't believe some girls walk partially naked right before my eyes. Most of the girls shave their legs and armpits too, and mine—well, I think my legs look like a grizzly bear. I won't even mention what my armpits look like because since puberty placed hair there, nothing has uprooted them. Two patches of thick shrubs. I'm a lot embarrassed to wear my shorts and lift my arms. I do know how to take care of the shrubs and the grizzly legs. I try shaving my legs with a razor, but I cut one of my legs when the cheap razor slips from my fingers. I won't try that again. I've seen other ways of shaving on television commercials.

I tread to the drug store after school one day and buy wax from pocket money Mama gave me. At home, I take one of Rose's small pots and with wax in my hand the pot is ready for the hot stove as the wax is ready for the hot pot. I don't bother to waste my time and read the label. It's a simple task. The wax will melt and I will spread it all over my legs. In no time, the solid wax bubbles like lava and is ready for grizzly-legs. I rush to the bathroom and spread the wax all over my legs, well from below my knees to my ankles, an act only a stupid newcomer can conceive.

Now, I cannot take it off. Well I can but only if I torture myself. I'm not supposed to spread the wax all over my legs like a cast over broken legs.

My talent for self-torture or to put it mildly, self-experimentation, is quite impressive. Why do I do stupid things all the time? Remember when I ran away not knowing if I would see my father? Remember when I slept at Amanda's house? Remember when I tested Mr. Bartley's shaving powder? Remember when I put on my Canadian shorts and didn't have anywhere to stay? Remember when I took that book to school? Remember when I didn't listen to Mama and talked to Robert? Remember when I hated Mama because she didn't want anything bad to happen to me?

It's almost two hours since I started my wax peeling adventure and I'm still groaning from my self-torture, sitting on the toilet seat in the bathroom, peeling away dried wax from my hairy legs ever so carefully, slowly, and painfully. The hair and dried wax leave a nice swollen reddish-shine. I won't even think about spreading wax over my armpits. And, dear Lord, now I'm trying to remove the wax from the pot but it won't go. What am I going to do? I've ruined my sister's pot. What will I do with it? Well, a brilliant idea now gives me the answer. Hide the pot and hope that a miracle will rearrange some of Rose's thoughts and she'll never ever remember that this little pot now dried with wax ever existed.

I must profess that with what I'm experiencing at school now makes having hairy legs and armpits a minor infringement in Canada. A freckled-faced, red-haired classmate wants me to feel ashamed of my name.

"Ha, ha, ha. Peaches." The kid laughs aloud every time the homeroom teacher calls my name.

Peaches, the name, the new student, and the shy kid live only for weeks in my new high school. I march into the school's office after class.

"I want to change my name," I say.

"Why?" the secretary asks.

"Because a kid in my class laughs at my name all the time."

"Peaches is a beautiful name. Don't change it. We love it."

"I want to."

The next day I tell all my teachers to call me Denise. I now feel like a stupid kid with a fruit name.

~~ ♦ ~~

A mesh wire fence separates the schoolyard and the yard of the building where I live, but there's a tiny opening between both yards that I squeeze through to walk to and from school. During lunch breaks, I squeeze through the fence to get home instead of walking on the main road where the other students walk.

On a bright September afternoon, I run home to eat my lunch. Mama is home. She's doing the laundry. While I eat, the phone rings and I run to answer it.

Report from Jamaica

"Peaches," John says and breathes loudly. Nothing else.

I know something is wrong. I just know it, but I don't know what it is.

"Yes," I say, waiting to hear what it is.

"Papa's dead."

I pause, there is nothing to say or I don't know what to say, then a loud and long wail bursts from my belly. And just as it came so sudden, it stopped. I don't know what happened to the phone in my hand, how it got to Mama. Mama talks to John. She doesn't cry.

I wanted to see my father again. Even just once. I wanted to hug and touch him. I wanted to see his face and his smile. I wanted to talk to him again. I wanted a new memory. But he's gone, only a few months after I left Jamaica. I don't cry again. Granny used to say, "What you never had, you will never miss." Maybe the saying is true, but, it's not about missing him. It's about not being able to see him again.

~~♦~~

As autumn approaches, I enjoy the view of trees showing off their leaves that color the sky and the earth. I'd never seen so many leaves change color like that, and I've never seen so many leaves fall on the ground before and I've never seen so many trees so naked—if they weren't dying.

Then I wait for winter and I wait for the snow because I've never seen real snow or felt it. Another afternoon, as I leave my class to go home for lunch, It comes. Snowflakes. The weather person calls it snow flurries. It's light. It floats in the air. I open my arms and turn my face to the sky. The flurries brush my face and evaporate. Then, the flurries change to heavy snow that covers the ground. This is beautiful.

Early the next year, in my homeroom class, my friend, the only person I'm close to and who has a fruit name too, Cherry, says, "Miss, it's Denise's birthday."

What do I do now? I'm thinking I'm the oldest in my class. Most kids graduate at seventeen or eighteen if they take the one year pre-requisite to go to university.

"Happy birthday, Denise," the teacher says. "Are you sweet sixteen?"

"No," I say.

"Are you sweet seventeen?"

I shake my head.

"Are you eighteen?"

I shake my head again.

The teacher doesn't know what else to say and I'm dying of embarrassment. I'm in grade eleven and I'm nineteen. No one knows why I'm in high school now, but I know they all think the same thing. I'm slow. I'm stupid. I repeated grades. I do feel stupid. I want to complete high school. That's all.

With everything and my feeling of being stupid, I quit going to school. I'm a serial quitter now. Three times. No graduation. I'll never fulfill my dream to graduate. I'm surprised that Mama and Rose aren't mad as I thought they would be. Of course, they're not happy, but they do not get angry about my decision.

Mama's factory job lays her off and she finds work as a cleaner at a hotel. I quit church too because it's far and I don't have anyone to talk to about God any more. Everyone else in the house rarely goes to church.

One year later, I reenroll in another high school after repairing old post office machines in a warehouse and now while cleaning offices at nights. I want to get my high school diploma so I'll get a good job. I need an attitude, self-esteem, and personality boost. I'll become a different person than I was at the other high school. I will register using my right age, but I'll give my friends a younger age and I'll stick to Denise. Plain. Clear. Simple.

26
Protesters, Helicopters, and Soldiers

School is fun and my English and drama teachers love me. I write to Andrea all the time and she wants to come to Canada. John calls often. He wants to come to Canada too.

Mama and Mr. Isaac decide to knot themselves together and Mama is going to Jamaica to do so. They're taking Bridgette with them. After thirteen years together, I guess they want to make their relationship legal. I don't know what took them so long, but, anyway, most Jamaicans, especially the poor, don't get married. It's just not a big part of the general culture, but it's a big part of the rich people's and church people's cultures.

Andrea, John and other relatives and friends in Jamaica will join the celebration. A week after Mama's arrival, the ceremony takes place. It's not a big wedding, just one where they go to a justice of the peace and then celebrate later at home.

Report from Jamaica

Late evening, the phone rings. It's a call from Rose about a call from Jamaica.

"John is dead," Rose says.

"What? Nooooo," I scream.

"Yes."

I hang up the phone, fall on the bed, and weep.

~~ ◆ ~~

Report from Jamaica

John had bought tires for his car from someone else when John came to attend Mama's wedding. The police picked up John for questioning after they saw the new tires on his car. They took him to the police station. Two policemen interrogated John. One shot John.

Another report is that people living near the police station claim they heard John screaming, getting beaten up before the police shot him a couple times.

The most commendable report, another day, is that the villagers are angry. John was a good person. He troubled no one and the villagers are fighting for him because he can't. They protest for justice. Some chant, "No justice, no peace."

Through the night, with only axes and machetes, and as the rain strikes, the people labor to accomplish their mission before daylight, before the first bus travels through the village.

They chop down big trees with only axes. They gather big rocks—boulders, rolling them with bare hands. They pile old tires and start a blaze.

They block the road. The main road.

Transportation halts.

Old tires burn.

Rain beats down, but the fire still burns the tires.

The cop who claimed to kill John rushes home after work each day like a scared chicken as he walks with a guard.

Another report. The media pour in. What could have gone so wrong in this almost unknown, tiny village? The media want the story. They interview people, and even try to get thirteen-year-old Bridgette to talk. She cries and cries. No words.

"This is police brutality," one person says. "We want justice."

The government is angry too, but not about my dead brother. The government is concerned about getting traffic moving through the village again. The government calls for calm. The villagers resist.

Another report. The government calls upon the military. It sends out a loaded helicopter that rains down soldiers sliding from ropes and landing in the village as the helicopter hovers. Protesters scatter. The soldiers parade with their big outstretched guns. The soldiers hunt the villagers. The soldiers spray bullets to scare them. The soldiers harass and ill-treat innocent bystanders.

By the time the family from Canada arrives in Jamaica, the protest had died. The courageous people did not want to die, but they brought John's cause to the nation, they captured the government's attention.

At the morgue, tears drop as I stare at John's body, his beautiful golden skin, his handsome face—the ugly wounds. They murdered him.

I touch his body. Cold. It's real.

I run my hands across his chest.

They pierced his face with two bullets. He's really dead.

They killed John. They killed my brother. They killed him in the same police station where I went after the man came into my room.

Self-defense, the policemen declared. But John can't defend what happened before they sprayed bullets in his face, how he willingly went to the police station with them. John can't say that he wouldn't and didn't try to grab one of their guns as they alleged.

Mama's heart is broken as she blames coming to Jamaica to get married as the reason John died.

"It would have never happen," she says. "He wouldn't have come. He wouldn't have bought the tires that cost him his life."

I know Mama must remember what she often said, that "The upholder is as bad as the doer." Regardless of the reason they slaughtered him, John should have known better, better not to buy the tires.

~~◆~~

Halloween, 1987, three months after John's death, Mama stands at the bus stop waiting for the bus to take her home from work. In a split second, a car making a left turn and one going straight collide and one hits Mama, sending her to the ground where she lies unconscious. Paramedics, police, ambulance, and police cars reach the scene. The ambulance takes her to the hospital. That's the report.

We rush to the hospital to see Mama. To make matters worse, Mama has a blood clot in one of her legs that is cutting off blood circulation and oxygen. She's dying but I hope she doesn't.

The doctors work their miracle and eliminate the blood clot. As Mama's income is cut off while she learns—for months—to walk again with a broken and now mended knee cap, I quit high school three months before the end of my last term, before graduation even though I'm progressing in school. I work in a factory to take care of myself.

~~◆~~

The journey to bring John's killers to justice is long and painful. First trial. Mama travels to Jamaica. Postponed. Silly reason. Second trial. Mama travels to Jamaica again. Postponed. Another silly reason. Frustrated, Mama asks me to write a letter to the Police Commissioner in Jamaica. The Commissioner does not respond. People tell Mama to let it go, to forget about the lawyers because she will never get justice in Jamaica. They say the police and the lawyers are like peas in a pod and that they work together. They tell her she should not waste her money, but Mama wants justice for John. Finally, when the case is tried, the police officers are acquitted. Mama cries. I vow to write about it one day. Andrea says she'll leave vengeance to God. Someone asks if we wanted him to take care of the police officers.

~~◆~~

It's now six years since we've left Jamaica. Rose and her husband, Edward, bought a house. Mama has regained her ability to walk. She sponsors Mr. Isaac from Jamaica and they live together with Bridgette who will graduate from high school soon. Shernette reunites with her Jamaican boyfriend who now lives in Toronto. They marry. I see my big brother, Jason, every now and then because he also lives in Toronto.

Andrea yearns to join us in Canada, if only for a short time. We try a variety of ways to bring Andrea to Canada, but each attempt is unsuccessful. One immigration officer rejects Andrea's application to visit Canada. He says, "You will not come back to Jamaica if we give you a visitor's permit." Another time when Andrea applies for a visa, another immigration officer stamps her passport and tells her not to apply again for two years. Rose and I apply for permanent status for Andrea and her family. Canadian Immigration turns down our application. Andrea decides to go back to school part time and she opens her own clothing store. She hopes that with her education and business skill, she'll be able to sponsor herself to Canada.

~~◆~~

I'm twenty-five with a well-paid factory job. With Hector's River far away and long removed from my life, I am free to do what I want to do. I'm pregnant. This goes against all my childhood dreams. On top of being pregnant, I didn't ask for marriage because girls... well girls should let the boys ask.

Now I'm "paying the price" as Mama would say. I should have continued living for God. Although I'm stupid at times, I think I'm smart enough to figure this one. I know he's gone. I know I'll be a single parent because the person who planned to have this baby with me isn't writing or calling me as he used to. He lives in the US. When he loved me, the phone rang and letters and cards poured in. When I talk with

214

him now, that's when he calls, he says he's busy or that he didn't get the time to call. He's gone, I know he's gone.

My situation gets worse. My job will lay off a lot of people indefinitely and I'm on the list. So now, I'm searching for something to do after the baby is born because I don't want another unstable factory job. The baby is born, a boy, Dylan. He's my joy and comfort. But I cry in the shower all the time and at nights when he's asleep. I cry for Dylan because I know he will grow up like me, not having his father around. I'm sad because I feel sorry for Dylan and myself. I don't know how I'll raise a boy. I'm scared.

Just before Dylan's first birthday, I start a one-year program for kids who dropped out of high school. It's the best plan I could conceive to avenge my involuntary single-mother status. I have to get something for myself. Getting an education will be mine and mine only. If I complete this program, I will get to go to university and get my college degree.

I'm not the brightest person in this program—some students understand everything and they write papers like pilots flying jet planes—because some words seem like another language to me, but I'm working hard and I get help from the academic success center at the university, which helps me to complete the program successfully. Now I'm a university student. The first year is a big disaster. But I'm working harder now. Mama feels proud I'm attending university. She didn't believe I was really in university when I told her.

"What's that thing called that you said you're doing in school?" she asks every now and then. She always forgets and asks me again.

"Bachelor of Arts," I say.

"What's that?"

"I'm taking History courses."

"So that can get you a good job when you're finished?"

"Yes, I can become a professor."

Sometimes I leave Dylan with Mama, Rose, or Shernette when I need to study at the library.

I take a writing course and my writing professor tells me that I'm a good writer so I'm writing stories about my life. But I realize that my story is not complete without writing bits of Mama's story. My professor says my story is a mother-daughter story.

I'm now at the end of the second year of a four-year program. I'm going to visit Andrea this summer and I'm taking Dylan with me. I'll plan the trip with a cousin. It will be a blast. I think so.

27
Is The Doctor Right?

1995. I visit Andrea in Jamaica. She's thirty-five. My love for Andrea has grown much stronger since I left Jamaica. I visit her often. One night, Andrea and I stand before the mirror and stare at our half-naked bodies before we put on our nightclothes. We joke about our breasts. Then Andrea asks something.

"Do you see this lump?" Andrea holds her right breast.

"No, I can't see it."

"Feel it."

I touch Andrea's breast and feel a lump. "Gosh, Andrea, this is pretty big. It's like an egg. Didn't you notice it before?"

"Just the other day I noticed it. It must be an abscess or something."

"Are you crazy, Andrea? Do you know it could be cancer? You better go check it out as soon as you can." Andrea widens her eyes and stares blankly at me for a few seconds.

"You think it could be cancer?"

"I don't know, but a lump in your breast could be serious, especially that big."

~~◆~~

A biopsy confirms that the lump is malignant. Andrea has cancer in her right breast. Christmas, 1995, Shernette and her family visits Andrea. Summer, 1996, Rose and her family visits Andrea.

~~◆~~

"Peaches," Andrea's voice cracks, "the other one is swollen. It's hard, it's stiff, and it's spreading. She should have taken both of them. I went to see the doctor. She said I should make a will," Andrea cries.

"Hold on, Andrea," I say and press the mute button. I cry and take a deep breath. I wanted Andrea to call and say that she is fine and that the cancer had left her body after she had a mastectomy, chemotherapy, and radiation. I press mute again.

"Andrea, I'm back."

"Peaches, tell Mama, that I'm sick and I need her. Tell her to find out from Immigration if I can come to Canada for treatment. I need you guys."

"I will come soon. OK?"

~~◆~~

Andrea has a seizure. Andrea is hospitalized.

March 12, 1997.

I land at Norman Manley International Airport in Kingston, Jamaica, a week after Mama and after the family decides to take turns going to Jamaica in the following order: Mama, me, Rose, Shernette and Bridgette.

I meet Mama in the Port Antonio Hospital in Portland, in the female ward on the second floor. The hospital stands on a hill that overlooks the city's marketplace. Andrea lies on a bed in a long room with about twenty beds and a washroom at one end and a table at the other, where the nurses sit.

Mama crouches over my 37-year-old sister like a lion shielding its young. Andrea looks different from when I saw her in 1995. She no longer has long black hair. She has short curly hair with streaks of grey.

"Hi Mama, hi Andrea." I hug Andrea and look at her sad eyes. Those eyes that sparkled and shone, that made everyone laugh, where have they gone? She hugs me with weak hands.

"How are you, Andrea?"

"I'm fine. I'm glad to see you."

"How is it?" I stare at her one swollen breast protruding from under her clothes.

"It's still hard. But it's getting a little softer because I got more radiation." I reach out to touch Andrea's breast. I pull my hand back.

"You can feel it." Andrea holds my hand and I gently touch the engorged, lumpy breast. I slide my hand gently over her chest to the side where the right breast was taken. Solid. Bumpy. Cold sweat chills my body and goose bumps rise on my arms. I feel nauseous.

"Oh An—drea," the words force from my lips, "How do you cope with this? Your chest, and your shoulders—like a rock."

"It was worse."

The cancer has metastasized beyond Andrea's neck. I move my hand upwards and feel her sunken, tight, twisted neck.

"Rub my neck," she whispers. I look at Andrea's eyes and see them begging me to help her. I take Q-tips, dip them in olive oil and stroke her neck.

~~◆~~

I don't want to faint while I am with Andrea. "I'll be back," I say and run outside. I run to the nurses at the front of the ward. "Can you help my sister? Please."

The nurses fix their eyes on me and say nothing. Maybe they do not understand me. I stare back at them. I repeat, "Can you help my sister? Pleeeease."

"We are doing our best," one says in a stern voice.

I run outside to the balcony again. I look below. I see a man with a white coat on. "Doctor! Doctor!" I shout. The man looks up at me. "Can you save my sister? Pleeeease. Pleeeease."

"I will come to see her later." The man walks off. I stop my tears and blow my nose.

Two days later Andrea talks about going to Canada for treatment. Andrea asks that I go to the oncologist in Kingston to get the documents for her to come to Canada. She asks Tanya, her friend, to travel with me.

~~◆~~

I leave Tanya outside the doctor's office because I do not want her to know anything bad about Andrea. I ask the doctor about Andrea coming to Canada. He says he would contact another doctor about that.

I ask, "How much time she has left?"

"If she makes it beyond three weeks it would be a miracle," the doctor says.

Tears pour from my eyes and I feel weak and I say that my sister is not going to die and I say goodbye and I walk to the door and the doctor says something and I cannot hear the words and I run into Tanya's arms and she hugs me and her tears wet my shoulder and she asks in a whisper what the doctor said and I tell her and ask her not to tell anyone and we put on our sunglasses.

~~ ♦ ~~

I meet Mama on the street. She looks tired. She wants to get the last bus to go home to Hector's River, where she stays, where Andrea lived with her family. After preparing fresh carrot juice and coconut water for Andrea each morning, Mama travels twenty-five miles to see her.

"Mama," I say and walk fast to meet her.

"What did he say?" she says.

"If she makes it beyond three weeks it would be a miracle." We stand on the busy sidewalk in Port Antonio. We hold each other. Mama's tears drip on my arm.

People pass by. Taxis, cars, vans and buses push through the crowd on the street. Drivers blow their horns to get people out of the way. Behind us people sell fruits, vegetables, fish, clothes, and crafts on the sidewalk and in the market. The smell of the foods in the market fills the air. A woman beckons a passerby to buy her fruits. "They cheap. Don't cost much. Give me a break, please." Another woman shouts, "Don't feel-up, feel-up my stuff if you not buying." A man stands with paper money in his hands and shouts, "Foreign currency. American dollar, Canadian dollar and the mighty British pound. I give you more than the bank."

Mama wipes her eyes and her nose and slowly pulls from me. I look at her and hold her hands. "We can't tell her, Mama. We can't," I sob. "She's not going to die."

~~ ♦ ~~

Each morning I climbed one hundred and twenty-one steps to see Andrea and descended the steps at night. I now walk toward the hospital and climb the steps again to see Andrea. "One… ten… thirty-three… eighty-two… one hundred… one hundred and twenty-one." I breathe hard. It is easy to climb one hundred and twenty-one steps when I think of my sister. My beautiful sister. My dearest sister. My sister who once loved me more than she loved herself. My sister who can make darkness as bright as day, who brightened other people's lives—she's leaving, us—. Why? Why? Why my sister?

Andrea sits on the balcony in a blue wheelchair. She wears her white cotton nightgown with a pink heart in the center. A pink towel wraps around her neck. I wave and smile at her with pain in my heart.

How do I tell her? What should I tell her? Should I tell her?

Yesterday we laughed and laughed. I saw sparkles in her eyes when she joked. "I feel like a fowl that someone has hit in the head," she said, "just spinning, spinning." Mama, Tanya and I, sitting around her bed, burst with laughter, and when I thought she would stop joking, she said, "My one breast, my only breast feels like a half-ripe breadfruit that needs roasting." We laughed again.

No. I won't tell her. I can't tell her.

I glance at her again.

She smiles. I know she thinks I'm bringing her good news.

I smile and wave my hand again.

"I'm back, Andrea," I shout.

I meet Andrea and hug her. "I hate leaving you alone." I hold her hand and kiss her forehead.

Andrea feebly holds my hand and gasps for air. She can't wait to hear the news.

"I - thought - about - you all - all day, Peaches," she says. "What, what - did he say?"

I look at the pink heart on her nightgown. I can't make her sadder. "He said he will prepare the documents for you to take to Immigration Canada when you are better."

~~ ◆ ~~

I gaze at the ceiling as I lie on the bed where I stay. I think about the lie I told Andrea today. *Does she believe me? Will she die? Is the doctor right? Am I wrong to think she will not die? Why Andrea? Where's God?* I close my eyes and feel tears pour and trickle down the sides of my face and wet the pillow. My heart hurts.

I picture Andrea as she recovers from her illness and as she waits for the letter of permission from Immigration Canada. I picture me running up the one hundred and twenty-one steps with the letter in my hand. I picture me taking the letter to her and watching her as her face brightens with—a look, maybe uncontrollable joy—an expression on her face that I have not seen before.

I open my eyes, blink and more tears flow. I wipe the tears, roll over on my belly—and. And—I see

Andrea on her neat, narrow bed, with a worn white blanket that covers her to keep her warm, with her blessed black Bible beside her pillow, with her bulky blue hymn book on the side table, with the old oxygen tank that stands on the floor beside her bed, with the opaque oxygen mask on her face and she sleeps serene, and—I don't want to think any more. I close my eyes and sleep.

~~ ◆ ~~

I tell Andrea I have to leave her with Mama because I have to write my exams so that I can get my Bachelor of Arts degree. I tell her I'll return once I write my exams and that I will stay with her until she gets better. I tell her Rose will come soon.

Andrea does not talk to me. She does not look at me. She does not hug me back. She does not say goodbye. She does not want me to leave. I cry because she will not say goodbye to me.

~~ ◆ ~~

A week later, after I return to Canada, Rose has an accident one day before she leaves to visit Andrea. She reports that while driving home from work after the night shift, she lost control of her vehicle and it spun out of control and flipped over. We almost lost Rose. But with willpower to see her once bubbly sister, Rose ignores her injuries and wearing big dark sunglasses to mask the swelling and the big black circles around her eyes, she boards the plane for Jamaica the next morning.

Report from Jamaica

The day she arrives in Jamaica, Rose stays with Andrea until late in the night. They talk. They laugh. They share memories. Early the next morning, like Mary searching for Jesus, Rose leaves out early to find Andrea. She wanders in the hospital room. She pulls the curtain that encloses Andrea's bed. A nurse stands beside Andrea's bed. A white sheet covers Andrea. From head to toe. Silence. Shock. Rose backs out the room. Tears pour behind her sunglasses. On her way from the hospital, walking down the hill, Rose meets Mama as Mama climbs the hill to the hospital.

Mama looks at Rose's face and the way she walks. Mama knows. They hug and cry on the street.

~~◆~~

Andrea had told me that she wanted us to bury her in Bottom Church's cemetery. We inform the church and there, we rest Andrea's body beside the church and before the sea. She'll like it there. She'll listen to the singing, preaching, testimonies, and confessions.

The ones left behind, father, brother, and sister died. And scarier, John and Andrea died ten years apart and the years ended with the number 7. 1987 and 1997. And Mama almost died from the car accident and the blood clot.

Shernette and I grow fixated on the ten-year death-wait and the digit, seven. I know that we'll go someday, but I'm not ready. How do we stop this? Who'll be next in 2007?

28
We Can't Stop it

1999. We can't stop it. We can't stop death.

We're now at the hospital waiting for Mama—Jason, my big brother, Rose, Shernette, Bridgette and me. The doctors are operating on Mama's thyroid. One has come to update us on the surgery and, well—the thyroid part of the surgery went well, but now, something else will change our lives again.

The doctor found cancer in Mama's thyroid. Our fears are real. There'll be another death. But he reassures us that thyroid cancer is easy to treat.

Mama will be OK, I guess. She has a tube down her throat and she cannot talk. We joke with her and tell her that for once she cannot talk and must listen to us. She smiles with heavy breathing coming from the tube. We're sad for Mama. But after a radioactive iodine treatment, with Mama locked in a hospital room for a couple days, and more visits to the doctor, Mama says she no longer has cancer. We believe her. After all, Mr. Isaac had prostate cancer in 1995 and now it's gone. So who's next if it's no longer Mama on the ten-year death list?

Report from Jamaica

2002. Andrea's son, Owen, is somewhat disconnected from reality. He frequents Parade, Kingston. He is dirty and wears ragged clothes. He begs for money. Reports are that he has been to the airport a couple times waiting for his mother, Andrea, to come and get him. The family sends money to help care for him and Rose decides to go to Jamaica to help take care of him. Before she leaves Jamaica, with medication from the doctor and someone to help care for him, Owen is nursed back to good health. The family, especially Mama, sends money to care for him.

Report from Jamaica.

2003. Owen tells some friends that he is tired and goes home to sleep. He does not wake up. We connect with Steve, Owen's dad, and together we pool our resources and bury Owen in May Pen cemetery where I used to pick plums when I lived in Trench Town.

~~♦~~

Two years later, 2005, Mama is in the hospital. The nurse begs her to tell us. Tell us what? Mama will not tell us. We have no idea what "tell us" is about. She's in the palliative wing. Most of the people here are dying. The doctors bring end of life papers for Mama to sign, and to make her will. She can hardly breathe. Maybe she'll die before 2007. After the nurse leaves and with us, her children, around her, and Mr. Isaac at home, Mama reluctantly does what the nurse tells her to do.

"I have the thing," she says in a calm voice.

"Cancer?" we ask.

"Yes, it came back. I didn't want to worry you. Don't tell anyone. You hear me. Not even Isaac. I don't want him to worry."

We cry.

That's Mama. Mama didn't complain that she couldn't feed us when she couldn't. She didn't say bad things about my father. She didn't pity herself. She did what she had to do in the best way she knew how.

As I wait for Mama in the hospital to get released, the nurse brings a report for Mama to take to another hospital. The cancer has metastasized to her lungs, making her breathing difficult.

~~ ♦ ~~

"You're the only one left," Mama says.

I know she's telling me that I should get married. I can't do much to make Mama happy in the marriage department. Even if I could buy her a house and take her around the world, she would not be satisfied that one of her daughters is not married. It's not that I couldn't have gotten married here in Canada, and it's not that I've been a saint or a recluse in the land of love, but it just didn't happen. For one reason or another, I inflict pain and others inflict pain. I love and leave and they love and leave me too. I walk away without looking back and others do the same to me. It's a vicious game out here—the playing with feelings, the breaking of hearts, the continuous search for perfection.

I must be sure that it will last—marriage—or I must make myself believe that whoever I marry will stay with me, will understand me, will accept my crazy ways. I must love him and know that he loves me too. It's hard to find a man who can love me the way I need him to love me. I think I'm too insecure and injured, too independent and uncompromising. And I've been on my own for too long.

And now, at forty-three years old, I have committed myself to be content with my life. I'm even pondering a life of sexual celibacy. After a long and sometimes difficult journey in university, I am now financially stable working as professor and a consultant in the field of education. I think I know the love-you-until-I-don't-want-to-any-more games we or people play, and I don't want a part of it any more. And I know that until-death-do-us-part isn't always true.

If marriage happens, that's OK. But now I'm not in any haste even though marriage was one of the goals I sent out to the universe. I love Mama so much that I want her to be happy for me, for her children, for the legacy she will leave even if that includes being a strict and not so perfect parent. I would love to get married and to make her happy, but I won't get married just to make her happy. I have to do it for me and for the other person included.

Over the years, Mama and I have grown closer. I call her almost every day and even if I have nothing to say, I just want to hear her voice and let her hear mine. I want her to know that I love her, love her more than ever before.

2007. A friend invites me to join Facebook. I don't want to go on Facebook just to show off or show pictures, which most people do. There must be a deeper meaning to being there. For now, though, with no vision to help make the world a better place I join Facebook.

April 2009, while checking my Facebook account one Saturday morning, I see an email:

Is this Denise from Jamaica?

After seeing who sent the Facebook email, without wavering, I reply.

Sure, how are you?

Next day.

Peaches, it has been a long time since Seaside primary. I see u haven't changed much.

Still beautiful as usual. Send me a number that I can call. Mine is [###########].

How is your sister and family?

With overwhelming joy, I call Grant, my first love. He knows me as Peaches and Denise. He lives in the US according to his Facebook profile. I can't wait to tell him what happened two weeks ago.

After saying our greetings, I explain what happened in my class.

"Two weeks ago I told my students the story about us in grade six. I had never before told anyone about us," I say.

"A few weeks ago I started thinking about you too. I even asked someone for your number but didn't get a response after waiting for it. I started thinking that I should try to find you some other way."

"Oh my God," I say. "We were connecting telepathically."

230

"Yes, I started searching on Google and when I couldn't find you, I went to Facebook."

"I can't believe this. I kept talking about you. We were connecting."

Grant then says he works for McDonald's as a Regional Training Manager and I couldn't believe him more.

"I'm a teacher, Grant. And do you know what I tell my students, friends, and family?"

"No."

"I tell them that if I were to get married, I wouldn't hold a big wedding. I say that I just want to go through McDonald's drive through and get married while ordering a happy meal."

"Serious?"

"Yes. This is the connection. McDonald's has come to me. I can't believe this."

"Believe it," he says. "I'm as real as McDonald's."

"What does this all mean?"

"It means we are meant to be with each other."

Grant tells me about his past life, that he's divorced and has two children. He wants to know if I still love him. I say yes, of course, that I still love him, but I'm afraid of committing to anyone.

We talk as though we have been friends all along. I explain why I didn't want to talk to him again in grade six. And despite the talks about marriage and telepathic connection, I tell Grant I'm not interested in a relationship but that I want to remain friends with him. Still, deep inside my heart, I love Grant but I'm afraid of giving him my heart.

Before we say goodbye, Grant says, "Peaches, I don't care where you are, where you live, or who you're with, I'll find you and marry you."

"Yeah, right," I say.

"Watch me," he says. "We were meant to be. This is not us. It's divine intervention."

"Will you come on a big white horse and get me?" I teased.

"Anything you want."

~~ ♦ ~~

When we meet, two months later, in a hotel parking lot in Toronto, with one glance at him, I am hypnotized. Grant has mighty *O-my-Jesus* muscular arms, flat stomach, and a roundish bald-head. His presence is magnetic, making me want to jump in his arms. But we promised each other that we will not touch, hug or kiss each other, and we will not encourage gazing in each other's eyes when we meet.

Suddenly and erratically, we break our promises as Grant walks over to me and the power of love sweeps us. We hug tightly. Our lips lock. We say nothing as our lips part. We are lost, unable to think with our minds, but we do with our hearts.

~~ ♦ ~~

Grant takes me to the CN tower in Toronto for my birthday dinner nine months later. As the dessert arrives, the waiters and chefs gather around—camera waiting and Grant on his knees with a ring in his hand. I cannot wait for the dinner to end to go home and share the joy.

Here is the letter I sent after.

Hello Relatives and Friends,

I want to share my engagement story with you in

pictures and words. Please see below and the slide
show.
[Grant] Ledwidge and Denise Clarke
Engaged January 22, 2010
Wedding destination and date not finalized
Wedding will be small
We want to spend time to work on our marriage plan
Not the wedding

Back Story
April 12, 2009, [Grant] contacted me
After thirty-two years, when we last spoke
When he wanted to know
Why I did not want to be his girlfriend any more

See, we were young
Eleven
In grade six
[Grant] did not know
That I drew a picture of him-my husband
And our little girl
I named her Samantha Ledwidge
And named myself Denise Ledwidge

The big bully in class
Who had been taunting me for a while
Found our little girl
When [Grant] was not around
The bully taunted me more
She showed our daughter
To some other students in our class
And my secret love life was discovered

233

So ashamed and embarrassed was I
I did not talk to [Grant] again
He did not know why
And he gave up trying to know
For years he wondered
Curious about what had happened

The tall, handsome and lanky young boy
With sun-burned red hair (yes he had hair)
Whom I talked about love with
Whom I walked to primary school with
Who once gave me a peck on my cheek
And held my hands

Would be a buried memory
Until early April 2009
When, for reasons I could not comprehend
He entered my mind again
And I spoke about him
Told my class about him
About what happened in grade six
Not realizing we both were
Reaching out to each other in this universe

A few days later
After a long search
To find me on the Internet
Just five minutes before his computer died
April 12, 2009, to be exact
I received a note from him
And immediately felt
The magical connection again

I quickly responded

And...
We spent many hours on the phone
He told me that I would be his wife
That it didn't matter whom I was with
Or where I lived
He would come for me one day
And take me away
And we would get married
And live together until death parts us
I said, "Yeah, right...."
And he said,
"Watch me. We were meant to be.... This is not us —
it's divine intervention...."

We dated when we could
But I did not know
How our story would end
Maybe in the far future
But December 2009
Surprisingly, I got a call
That he would spend Christmas with me
And I knew at that moment
That what he had said would certainly be true
And we would be together -- for sure

We met each other's families
We got approval from them
They gave their blessings too
Everything felt so surreal
Yet so right
The way it was intended to be

I had waited for him
For my whole life

Every seemingly disappointment
Tears, pain and heartache
Now indeed were parts of my journey
Back to him
For I could not be happier
With anyone else, I'm sure
But the person I now affectionately call
[Grant] Pow-wow
And who calls me Peachy-Pow

Mama gets her wishes. One month later, I move to the U.S. to live with Grant. We marry, not at McDonald's but under a gazebo, in a park, and near a lake in Pennsylvania.

Mama is happy. She is so happy. Mr. Isaac is happy too.

"I'm so glad you found someone," Mama says.

"He's a good boy," Mr. Isaac says.

Grant found me, but it doesn't matter how Mama sees union with Grant. I know the meaning of her words.

My marriage joy is mixed with the sadness that comes with Mama's illness. She will visit us in Pennsylvania, but she can't stay too long, she might not survive the eight to ten hour drive from Toronto because of the blood clot in her lungs. Still she's determined to come and see where I live. I hope she'll survive the trip.

29
In This Moment

2010. Mama arrives in Pennsylvania with Rose's three children. Mama admires the house I live in, the river below, and the railroad tracks behind. Like a child, she giggles and hurries to the patio to view the train when the train operator blows the whistle. I can tell the sounds that accompany the oncoming train are as musical instruments to her ears, not the harsh scraping, clanging, rattling and thunderous sounds that annoy me sometimes.

Mama seats herself on a patio chair. She finds joy and comfort in this moment. This moment of the passing train, the harmony of the thundering, jarring and piercing sounds. She finds joy and comfort. For she stares with child-like gaze, smiling as she counts and counts the number of cars the train carries. Before her visit, I had not seen that kind of beauty in the passing of a train, although I always told Grant that the love train was passing through whenever one squeaked or clanked as it chugged by the house.

Together, Mama and I, in this moment, no longer as mother and daughter, more like childhood friends, bond as we count freight train cars. We bond like children playing a counting game. We gasp in awe when the train stretches out—long, squeaking, scrapping, rumbling—ceasing to end and we count and count. One hundred and twenty, this one.

"That's a long one," she says.

"Yes. Wow. Yes."

"One hundred and twenty."

"I didn't know these trains carried so many cars. So long. Thanks, Mama. If you didn't start counting them, I wouldn't know."

Mama can only stay for two weeks. The blood clot in her lungs dominates her life more than the cancer.

"So *The Thing* was there doing nothing and nobody knew," she once said. "Then this lump came up, and it said, I'm going to show people that I'm here, so they'll know."

We laughed.

"Then the blood clot came, and it said, I'm the baddest. You have to pay attention to me."

"I know," I said.

"Now both of them in the lungs." Cancer and blood clot.

"But you're doing fine," I said. Words to console her.

Mama has to do bi-monthly blood monitoring that determines if she needs to reduce or increase the anticoagulant, or blood thinner, she takes daily.

Today. We stroll to the pool. We splash in the water. I don't know why I see Mama as a child. Maybe because she's helpless with the cancer. Maybe because I want new memories with her. Smoothly, she swims so smoothly, so in control of herself and the water. I try to imitate her, but I can't. I try to swim, but I splash as someone losing control, drowning, sinking to the bottom. She laughs and shows me what to do, but I'm a klutz. *I'll never swim with her.* She didn't teach me and I didn't learn, I still can't learn even with Grant trying his best to teach me. Some things, I know, I may never learn.

In everything she does, it's hard to forget that this cruel monster lives inside of her. So I like to cherish the moments I have with her. I've learned that mothers are precious, that my mother is precious and because I'll lose her sometime soon, I love her even more. And I know that in her own ways, she loves me too.

Another day. We travel to Philadelphia and leave her and Mr. Isaac with some of Grant's family members while my nieces and nephew tour the city with Grant, Rocky Balboa statue included in the tour. Mama can't cure her cancer by exercising, by persistence, by faith as Rocky Balboa in the movie by the same name. She has faith, she has been exercising, walking five days each week for the last nine years. She tries to eat right too, and take herbs to cure it. But, there's no good food or workout routine or faith that will save her now. The cancer is here to stay. It is.

We travel back to Toronto with her and Mr. Isaac, stopping as often as we can to let her walk and circulate her blood. I often wonder what she thinks. Will this be her first and last visit to Pennsylvania?

Will she make it for a few more months, possibly a year? More? I'm not sure.

~~ ◆ ~~

January 2011.

"Should I get chemotherapy again?" Mama asks me on the phone.

The oncologist says Mama has about a year to live. I want to trust him because the oncologist was right in Andrea's case. I don't want to live on a false dream. Mama knows better not to. We have seen Andrea, we didn't want to believe. I can't give Mama false promises. She has too much experience. We did that with Andrea. I don't ever want to do that again.

Chemotherapy was bad for Mama. Her complexion changed. She lost her appetite. She lost weight. She grew discolored fingernails and toenails. Now, the cancer has metastasized even more. More chemotherapy will only prolong her life for a short time with devastating effects and might affect her worse than the first time. I can't encourage her to suffer more discomforts only for a few more months of life.

Mama pondered about my life. Now I ponder about her life. She didn't want me born into a life she could not support and I don't want her to continue living a life of discomfort. Mama has to make that decision because she knows the pain.

"Mama, remember how you felt and what it did to you," I say. "I wouldn't do it again, but if you want to, then go ahead. I'll support you."

"So this is it."

Mama's voice is soft and sad. "So this is it."

She will not prolong her suffering.

It hurts to respond to "So this is it." She's saying it's final, her days are numbered. I don't respond because I won't tell her any phony stories just to make her feel better. She'll know I'm lying anyway. This is not our first case. We're not naïve about *it*.

~~◆~~

I remember when I travelled with Mama for radiation treatments. She sat with hope and bravery. And we laughed when I told her she looked like Spiderman when she donned her radiation cast. I remember that Mama had a peculiar appetite when she had an appointment at Princess Margaret Hospital, Toronto. She asked for a hot sausage or a hot dog after her appointments. When the hospital, Sunnybrook or Trillium admitted her, late at night, she asked one of her daughters or any of the grandchildren to sneak in McDonald's Fillet O' Fish and fries. It was scary but fun-filled as we sneak by the nurses and tiptoe in her hospital room with McDonald's. Those foods, as I look back, comforted her as she faced her fears after seeing doctors.

After denying Andrea from eating certain foods because we thought we could heal her with a different kind that didn't work, we never stopped Mama from eating "treats" after her visits to the doctors. I still see Andrea's sad eyes begging for the food we denied her. I remember when Mama left her chemotherapy treatments—not complaining—she didn't ask for a hot dog or a sausage. Chemotherapy robbed that craving.

As the clock ticks, her life nearing its end, Mama calls me and she laughs as she talks about her trip to the hospital. She cannot walk as fast as she used to. Rose pushed Mama in her walker as if she were in a wheelchair and they laughed as Rose zipped passed people on University Avenue to get to the doctor in time.

~~◆~~

I arrive in Toronto, surprising Mama. Her spirit lifts and she feels happy to see me. I give of myself to her, all that I can and relieve my sisters of the work they do for her when I'm not here. Breakfast, lunch, dinner, I give with love. I redecorate her bathroom.

She prays at five in the morning, a long pleading prayer, asking God to protect her but to let His will be done. She prays with a hunger for life in her voice, and an urgency, a cry for more time. I hear the pain in her voice. I sense the sadness given to her by her illness. She cries and asks God to watch over her children—us—when she's gone, to guide and protect us, to give us joy and happiness, and to give us good health.

As I drive back to Pennsylvania, the gray sky pours rain. I cry. And I'm glad that, as tears wash my face, rain pours over my car and shrouds my face, my crying.

There's so much to cry for. Mama is not the same. She can't walk to see me out the door any more. She's "drugged-up." Morphine all day and laxatives—three different kinds—to aid the side effects of the morphine. Morphine is all the doctors can give now. The morphine talk is cliché as I heard it from the nurses and the pharmacist too.

"At this point we care about the quality of your life," they say.

"You don't need to live in pain for the rest of your life."

"This is the best we can do to make you comfortable."

Mama knows that the morphine will kill her more than the cancer because she takes it daily. She tried to resist taking morphine until... well, until the pain that goes into her spine, into her legs and her knees, became chronic, nagging and unbearable.

The rain stops. The drive through Syracuse seems better as the sky spreads brighter. The trees stand still in spring-bloom mode as small leaves decorate them in an array of green shades. I cry again as I reach into the bag for something to eat, the bag of snacks that Mama prepared for me for the road as I tried to leave the house in a hurry, to arrive home before night.

"God," I shout. "It's just you and me in this car. I pray that Mama will get better. Is that possible? Will you heal her? Is this her fate?"

I cry.

The land is green, the sky is clear, the road is wet, and my mind is sad.

I'll exit. I'll buy gas.

I'll see her again, soon, I know I'll see her again.

30
Waves Chipping Rocks into Sand

June. My dearest mama has less than three months to live. That's what the oncologist said. The cancer has finally devoured her whole body—organs to bones. A nice parasite it is—that cancer. It sneaks up on someone and at every opportunity, it plunders and monopolizes a whole body and poisons and paralyzes and kills all the living tissues it can and finally, it suffocates its prey.

With all the cancer, with all the doctor's visits, with all the blood monitoring, the uncertainties, nothing has shocked me more. It's really happening. Less than a year. Tears spew over and over. For a long time. Grant doesn't have any unique method to control my crying. He listens to me, sometimes. He hugs me, sometimes. I rest my face against his chest, sometimes.

I can't stop thinking about Mama.

Mama groans in discomfort, my sisters plan the funeral, and I prepare to take another trip. Maybe my last to see her.

Mid July, Mama tells Mr. Isaac for the first time that she has cancer. He cries about the inevitable loss. He cries like a baby—for days. Mama had begged us not to tell him because she didn't want him to worry. Mid July, Rose drives to the funeral home to make arrangements. Mid July, Bridgette calls crying that Rose went to make funeral arrangements without telling or including her.

Mama reports that Shernette gave her a candlelight bath and stayed with her at nights and they prayed and read the Bible together. Mama said Jason, the eldest child, brought her dinner. Bridgette took her young children to visit Mama and did the banking for her. Rose's children helped and every day, one made her oatmeal porridge. Shernette's children visited. Living many miles away, I can't take care of Mama as I want to. I have to go back to see her.

I tell Mama that I'm coming soon.

"How long will you stay?" she asks.

"As long as you want me to."

"Really."

"Yes, Mama. As long as you want me to stay."

Mama counts down the days before I arrive in Toronto.

"Four more days."

"Three more days."

"Two more days."

"Tomorrow. Tomorrow you'll be here," she says. I detect the smile in her voice. Her simple question and her simple child-like talk stir a deep pain in my heart.

245

In Toronto, I cry more when I see Mama, my mother, so tiny, so frail. Lord, I wish I could help. With the decline of her health, one by one the "accessories" move in to accommodate her, her pain, her discomfort. The walker. The first. The others follow: the bathtub handrail, the bath chair, the showerhead, the wheelchair, the hospital bed, the 24/7 working of the oxygen tank. And the hospice workers come: the doctor, nurses, personal care worker. People she talks with come: friends and family, pastor and church members. The services come too: the prayer meetings, the personal talks, the last communion. And the morphine in pill form comes: morning, noon and night, then by the hour, more and more and more morphine. And the well-wishing comes in different forms: postcards, flowers, money, phone calls, hello messages. Our family facing "this."

"I'm at peace," she says.

~~ ◆ ~~

Because she's weak, I—the whole family—try to encourage her to eat more as her appetite shrinks. Mama asks my niece to make her oatmeal and before she drinks it, she says, "This is the last." And we cry as that's all she drinks, though she has a few sips of water. The whole family tries to keep her alive. We know the math answer to cancer plus zero food.

I donned my must-save-her-attitude. Sometimes, only when you comprehend what's at stake, you fight hard to keep it. Mama's life is at stake. If she goes, we'll never see her again. More time is good and a nourishing bowl of soup should keep her going for a while. That's what I'll make for her today. I buy fresh vegetables and fresh chicken from the store and I prepare the most nutritious pureed chicken broth. It smells oh-so-good and tastes so delicious that even Rose and Mr. Isaac drink some. Mama will like it, and it may even revive her appetite.

I grab a tray and put the bowl of pureed chicken broth on it.

"This is for you, Mama," I say. "It will give you more strength."

Mama looks up at me, standing before her and, as I attempt to rest the tray on her lap, she smiles, I guess at my kind gesture and good wishes. Then, I can't believe it, she shakes her head to say no.

Stunned, tears roll down my face. "Please, Mama," I cry. "You have to eat—or else you're going to die. Please." I try to wipe away the tears but they spew wildly.

"OK," she says. "I'll drink it."

I sit beside her and observe her as she forces herself to please me. Late in the day, after she's long gone to sleep, I Google "symptoms when death is near in cancer patients."

I won't force her to eat any more. It will progress—worse. She'll lose all mobility, walking, talking, sitting, even seeing. She may lose all consciousness. But she'll still hear. I cry.

"I don't want to be hooked up to any machines," she says when we ask if she wants a feeding tube. "What's the use, if I can't eat?"

She asks only for ice or water and sometimes food that her mind probably tells her she needs, but her appetite says no when we offer her the food. She asks for ackee and salt-fish, the national Jamaican dish. But she doesn't touch it and I don't cry. I don't cry for her to eat any more.

Brushing her teeth, combing her hair, and washing her body—those are good for me to assist her, but they are not enough for me to do. I wish I could do more. Save her.

~~ ♦ ~~

I like our meetings—just Mama and me—I like our meetings. I love to take care of her, touch her when I can, make her happy. I like the way we communicate without saying much but communicate so much, with our bodies, our eyes, our touches. She's a brave woman, courageous, strong.

But I carry a burning question, one I know she may not want me to ask. But I feel I must. I need closure. Maybe I could tell her sorry and she could tell me sorry too. Just a simple answer will do. And in this moment of life and death, sadness and forthcoming loss, the question bounces back and forth in my mind as I don't know how to ask it.

I don't know what she'll say, how she'll react, where this will leave us. Will this harm how I see the end of her life or our solid friendship or our relationship as mother and daughter? Will I hurt anything?

She lies peacefully on her bed. Is this worth it? But what if she doesn't talk about it? Like she's done all these years. She ignores it, as if it never happened. Do I really need an answer?

Maybe, in this her final few months, days, maybe she'll talk to me. She doesn't know that I wait like a predator; that's what I really am right now because she's vulnerable. She's now Mama the sick. She never wanted to be like this, not ever, not even in her last days. She never wanted sympathy or help. That's how she is. She wanted to go strong, able-bodied, independent.

With the two of us alone in the room, this is the right time. The question has haunted me since the night of the beating. I shouldn't worry about asking because she is never afraid to speak or respond to her children, not even in her sickness. She knows I love her. And knows I would never hurt her. I guess I'm not taking advantage of her condition. I want to know before she leaves. But really, really, is this the time to evoke bad memories? This is a time to make her happy, for soon, soon this time we'll never have again. So why can't I let it go?

I love you Mama, I say to myself. But I must ask, even as a smile creeps over her face. And spreads softly. *Mama, I need to know.*

I gaze at her and ask, with pauses, afraid to rush the question or to throw it at her unexpectedly. Afraid to ask her.

"Mama," I pause. "Remember that night… you know… the night… the night when you beat me…."

Mama listens. No interruption.

"Why… why did you beat me?"

Mama gazes. The smile disappears. What will she say? I hope for her answer. I'll finally learn what happened the night that almost destroyed our relationship, forever. She furrows her brows, as though she feels pain, as though I've said something awfully abominable and she turns her face away from me and stares before her and shakes her head and I don't know what all the emotions mean, but Mama begins her response by throwing back a question to me in a harsh tone.

"Does someone do something for no reason?"

I turn my face from her, stare in my lap, and say nothing. I feel hurt. I hoped, even as I knew she probably wouldn't respond, I hoped we could talk about the past—the bad things, as we did about the good things. I wanted to talk about it.

She says nothing more. Nothing. And I don't know what to say. It's as if Mama just slapped me to shut up. I know she'll take the answer to her grave.

She knows. I know she knows that's not the answer I wanted. I feel ashamed, I feel ashamed that I asked her.

A smile of regret, something, nothing big—would be good enough from her. We could have talked or laughed. I don't know if she wanted me to forget the night. But I do know something. Yes, I know even as I stare in my lap, I know. I know Mama so well. I know that silence is all I will get and that's what she'll take to her other life. She's stuck in her past, her upbringing, her sorrows, her wounds, her history. She cannot talk about hurt. It's not something her parents did. They lived as though everything was alright.

Thirty years later and I still don't have closure. I had forgiven her a long time ago. Now I must focus on the fact that she's really dying, not now, but slowly. I love her as my mother and even with all that has happened between us, I would never trade my Mama for another mother. She did her best or what she thought was the best. She made mistakes, of course, she did. And of course, I know they are mistakes. But we can't change what happened in the past. But we can learn from our mistakes and we can heal the wounds of the past.

I guess, in many ways, I'm just like her. We don't change—my mother and I—some things we do not change. Forever the same. We will have to accept, or I have to accept that we both are always right. Stubborn. Strong headed. Not yielding even when we should. We stand firm as we beat against each other. Mama and I are predictable as day meets night and as obvious as laughs and cries. We are just like each other, too much like waves striking against rocks, waves chipping rocks into sand, sand falling in the water.

~~♦~~

The palliative care service sends a new accessory for Mama because she has difficulty swallowing her morphine pills. We do not want her to choke. The solution is a battery operated machine with tubes that connect a syringe that the nurse sticks in Mama's abdomen. It's called the pain pump. Every fifteen minutes it automatically releases the pain medicine, and when the pain is unbearable, such as when Mama tries to move, we press a button and it releases more pain medicine. It is potent, that's what I've read, but it surely takes away the pain. When Mama feels more pain, she does not press the button. She asks one of us to do so. Maybe she's afraid she'll press the wrong button.

~~♦~~

Some days we sit side-by-side on the sofa and hold hands. I love this. Now we sit in silence.

"Do you want to talk?" I say, afraid of saying something that will disturb her.

Mama and I are good at saying a single word that means a lot. Talk. She knows what talk means. All kinds of thoughts crowd my head, thoughts that can only be thoughts. I hope she has something to tell me that she hasn't said before. She told me a lot of things, especially when I used to go to work with her and last year and this year. As I gathered information for this book, I asked her questions. She liked to tell me the good things, not the bad.

But Mama won't say anything. "Not now," she says. "Later."

I'm thinking that she means later when she's about to die.

"Thanks for having me," I say.

"Uhnn." She utters with a smile.

"I'm glad you're my mother. I love you, Mama."

~~ ◆ ~~

Lord, I wish I could help. More. What's a life? What's a life when it comes and goes just like that? When you want to live but you're forced to die? When all dignity, pride, and autonomy are gone? "What's the use, if I can't eat?" she once said. God, I don't blame her. What's life when flesh melts from bones like starving humans in famine and lips crack as if there's no water supply and people come to stare at you as a spectacle, someone on display? What's a life?

~~ ◆ ~~

As we sit, holding hands, in one of her final days, she looks at me with child-like eyes and asks something that I do not expect. It's her turn to ask me a question. I listen.

"Does…." she tries to ask, but she's afraid. *Afraid to ask what?*

"What, Mama?" I look in her eyes. "What is it?"

"Does it…."

She's never been afraid to say or ask something. She's probably embarrassed to ask. I'm eager to hear. "Does it hurt?"

"What?"

I'm eager to answer her question.

"When you're…."

I think I know the word.

"Dying?" I ask.

She nods.

Though she's calm, though she's ready—she's scared. For all her display of bravery, courage, and humility—she's scared. She does not complain, she hides her fears. She, with grace, accepted what life handed her, poverty, me, troubles. But now, now she's scared, scared of the final moment, not because she's scared of death, but because she knows the torture that the cancer can inflict. She has felt and endured those gut-wrenching pains before. *God! Why? Why after all she's been through, just when life seems good for her, she loses her children and loses her life too? Why?*

I try hard to hold back the tears. I try to be strong for her. After a silent deep breath, I answer as I stroke her hand, the thin skin.

"No." I say as though I am certain. "I don't think so because you're taking the pain medicine." I point toward the pain pump. "It shouldn't, Mama. It shouldn't hurt."

She nods. "That's the only thing I was scared of. If it hurt." Her hand relaxes in mine.

"No. It won't." I hold my tears back.

Because I know Mama, I think this question is not about death or her last moments. She wants me to assure her that I won't let her feel pain. She's saying, *"If you see that I'm feeling pain, just press the pump."* It's Mama's way of communicating. Her words are always like parables or puzzles that we put meaning to or piece together. As her child, her daughter, I know her.

Four days later, with her in and out of consciousness, I hope and pray that Mama doesn't feel any pain. She doesn't talk any more. She cannot. The morphine and cancer have paralyzed her.

Daily, I sit by her bed and watch her chest as it moves. It rises and falls. I watch because I don't want to miss the last minute with her. I want to make sure she doesn't feel any pain. When she's ready to go, I want to hold her hand and tell her it's OK. Whenever I walk in the room, I watch her chest movements again. It's my way of guaranteeing that she's alive and not hurting.

Saturday. Mama cries out, "Peaches. Peaches."

I run to hear if she'll tell me what she promised to talk about "later." But that's it. That's all she said. She falls again into unconsciousness.

Sunday morning. We sit around her. We cry. We talk to her. She does not respond. We're scared. We do not know what to do. We call the doctor. We tell him we're are scared. We tell him we do not know what's happening or has happened to Mama. He assures us that Mama can hear us. He calms our fears.

He tells us to say good things to her and that we should not to say anything that will disturb her. Then, Andrea's daughter says, "Mama, when you see my mom, please say hello to her for me and tell that her that I'm sorry for the troubles I gave her." Suddenly, Mama opens her eyes. She gives a quick blank stare. Then, her eyelids lock again. I can tell she put a lot of effort into opening her eyes for this one second, to please us, and let us know she can hear us.

So happy are we that we stop our crying and we laugh and cheer her on and tell her thanks, but she sleeps again.

Sunday evening. After returning from taking my shower and talking with the pastor, the family, family-in-law, and the pastor, we gather in the room. I hurry to Mama's side because I feel I had left her alone, well, with Mr. Isaac, for too long. I walk up to her and I notice her dry lips. I turn away for a second to get Vaseline to moisten her lips. And just like that second that she opened her eyes this morning, in the second I turned away, her chest does not rise again.

I shake her. Tears well in my eyes.

I cry, "Mama, Mama... Mama isn't breathing."

~~♦~~

After the funeral, driving back to Pennsylvania, Grant and I drive up to the U.S. border guard.

"What was the purpose of your travel?" the guard asks.

"You don't want to know," I say. After the words leave my mouth, tears rain uncontrollably. Of course, Grant explains the rest and the guard quickly sends us off. For many miles after crossing the border, I cry.

~~◆~~

2011. Christmas. Grant and I return to Mama's home to celebrate the holiday. As Grant and I enter the house, I cry.

It's OK," Rose says, unable to hold back her tears.

"Don't make me cry more," I say.

Downstairs where she lived in Rose and Edward's basement, memories of her scatter everywhere: in the tidiness and neatness of the home, in the display of ornaments and pictures, and in the refrigerator and the cupboards. Memories of her scatter on the faces and gestures of my sisters. Memories show in the sadness in Mr. Isaac's eyes.

Last Christmas, red was the theme. A merry color. She danced with Mr. Isaac. Grant danced with her, too, though she pretended to be shy. I wonder if she had wondered about the possibility of not being here this Christmas. I had thought about this Christmas. We miss her. She knew we would miss her. She knew we loved her.

~~◆~~

Daylight brightens the room in the early morning as I lay awake beside Grant. And from nowhere, like a call in an open land, her voice comes clearly to me.

"Peaches. Peaches."

Lured by the call, a mother's voice, the beautiful voice, the voice I long to hear again, like a child, I ease off the bed trying to not to disturb Grant. I stroll slowly out the bedroom door and wander to find her. The voice. My mother.

"Mama," I whisper. "Mama, is that you? Is that you, Mama?"

I stop. I stand still. My eyes gaze around the living room. I wait to hear her voice again.

"Mama. Mama."

Nothing.

I feel something in my heart, a weakness, loneliness, sadness, emptiness. Pain.

I sob. "Mama, where are you?"

The house remains quiet.

I want her to answer, to hold my hand, and take me with her again, like the times we walked as mother and daughter, holding hands, laughing and talking as we walked over the hill and to the place where she worked, washing clothes. Those days are gone. Never again. Mama.

I roam back to the room. "What's wrong?" Grant says.

"I heard Mama calling me. I went to find her. She wasn't there."

"It's OK."

"She called me. I heard Mama's voice."

I rest my head on Grant's arm. I cry.

~~♦~~

"You know you barely made it into this world." I hear Mama's voice. She laughs. "But you're here and that's all that matters. And you gave me troubles not knowing that I only wanted to protect you. And that question you asked, the one that burned inside of you for many years, the one I didn't give you an answer to, don't worry. The closure you want is not in a verbal answer. It's in the many things we've done since then—my love for you, my trust in you, the happiness I want for you, the strong bond—even in death, that we still share. Closure isn't always words. So I've said it. Now go on. Live your life. Love your family. Take care of Isaac. Love your sisters and your brother. Love your husband and your son. Strive for happiness."

"Thank you for loving me, Mama," I say in my mind. "Yes, closure isn't always words."

About Day Laughs, Night Cries

Day Laughs, Night Cries: Fifteen is the first book in the Day Laughs, Night Cries series. Please visit www.daylaughsnightcries.com for upcoming release dates of other books.

We would like your feedback about our books, resources or products. Submit your feedback to us via our contact page on our website or send us an email at info@daylaughnightcries.com.

You can also find Peaches Ledwidge's blog at http://conceivewriting.blogspot.com/.

Healing wounds, one teardrop at a time

Tribute 1

Dear Mama,

I don't know how to start this letter, what words to say, but I'll begin
I don't know how to tell you, I'm so broken, so lonely within

You gave so much, you asked for little, even when life became unbearable
You toiled, you prayed on bended knees, even though your cancer was incurable

I haven't accepted the cursed illness, but I've accepted that leaving wasn't your will
I have cried many, many times, for some days I needed you still

You concealed most of the pain, most of the sadness, even as you tried to resist
You weren't always right or perfect, but perfection does not exist

I didn't have to search, I didn't have to fuss, you were my mother of grace
I praised you because you kept everything well, nothing out of place

You didn't tell me how to handle this when sometimes we never saw eye to eye
You remained silent, then you left, you didn't say

goodbye

I miss your face, your smile, you were the best you could be, my mother

I miss your voice and our talks, for there is no other

You knew you had to go, yet with all your inner strength, you went as a lamb

You taught me so much that made me who I am

I felt your love and your pain as I watched you lay and wither away

I love you Mama and remembering you makes a sad, sad day

Tribute 2

The Love We Share

I will never forget your happy face
Your big smile and sparkling eyes
Your contagious breath-taking spirit

I will never forget your fears and tears
Your joys, pains and sorrows
Your unspoken I-love-you

I will never forget the bond and love we share
The miles we run and the times we touch
The laughs we cannot stop

I will never forget all that we do
Even if you go
Because you are special

I will hold you in my heart
As I remember our love
And love you forever

For Marcia

Sources

Short Story
Clarke, D. (2003). "Marci-Pooh" in *Will You Still Love Me If I Shave My Head?* Toronto: Life Rattle Press.

Book
Clarke, D. (1996) *Waves Against Rocks and Other Stories.* Toronto: Life Rattle Press.

Blog

Ledwidge, P. (2011, September 19). Mama, Goodbye Mama. Retrieved from http://conceivewriting.blogspot.com/2011/09/so-she-sails.html

Ledwidge, P. (2012, February 15). The Love We Share. Retrieved from http://conceivewriting.blogspot.com/2012/02/love-we-shared.html

Ledwidge, P. (2012, September 18). Mother, You Didn't Say Goodbye. Retrieved from http://conceivewriting.blogspot.com/2012/09/mother-you-didnt-say-goodbye.html

Notes

www.ingramcontent.com/pod-product-compliance
Lightning Source LLC
Chambersburg PA
CBHW031951040426
42448CB00006B/312